# Freshwater Stingrays
# from South America

Richard A. Ross, M.D.

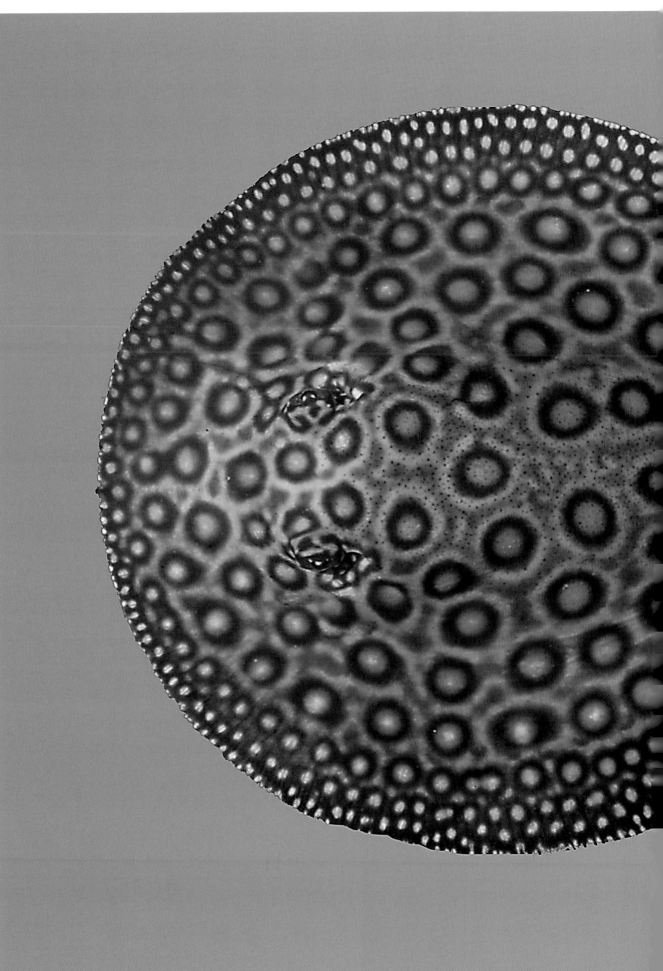

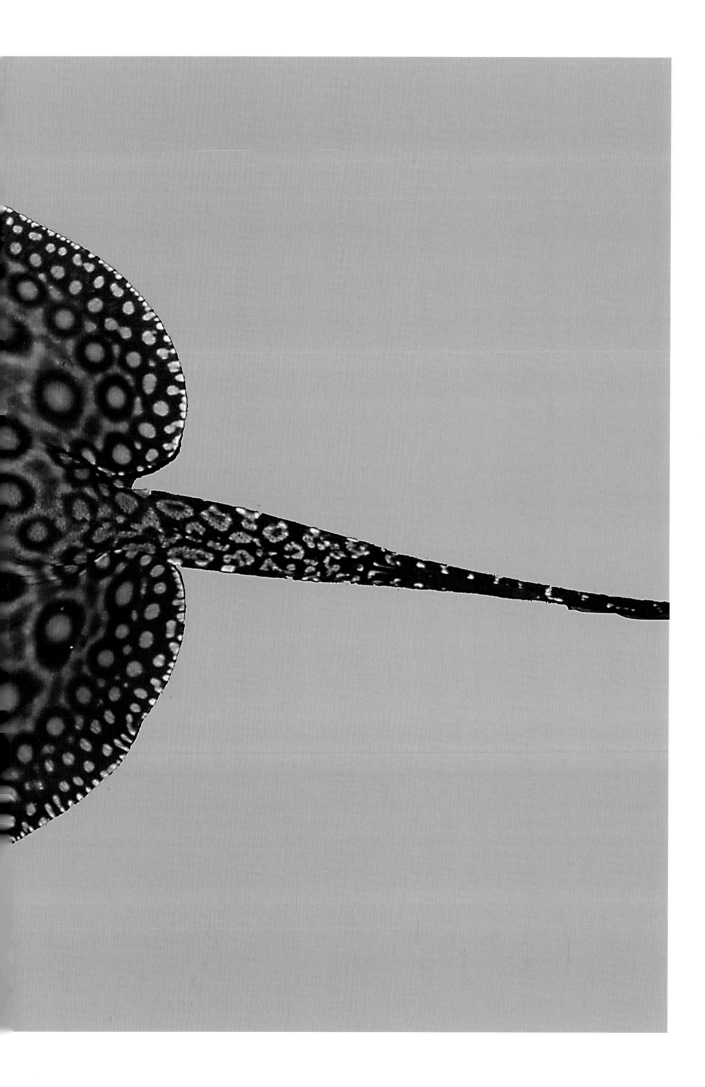

*The Author would like to express his sincere gratitude to the following people who have generously shared their experiences and advice. Without their contributions, this book would have not been possible: Dr. Labbish Chao, of Project Piaba, Dr. James Langhammer, Mr. Jose Mantilla, Mr. Oliver Lucanas, Mr. Fernando Torres, Mr. Harry Rambarran, Mr. Michael Rambarran, Dr. Peter Piermarini, Dr. George Benz, Mr. Christian Steimer, Dr. Nathan Lovejoy, Mr. Miro Espana, Mr. Harry Tsavtarides, Mr. Benjamin Rosler, and Mr. Steven Underwood. The author is especially indepted to Mr. Andrew Camoens, whose tireless effortsto expand our knowledge of stingray husbandry have added tremendously to this book. His work on the reproductive husbandry of stingrays is a major contribution to our understanding of these fish. I am also indebted to Mr. Yuuichi Muira for his expertise in digital technology that produced the photographs of reproductive behaviour of Potamotrygon motoro.*

*Above all, I am grateful to my wife Cathy for having the patience to let me bring so many weird and wonderful animals into our lives.*

All pictures by R. Ross if not mentioned otherwise.

We would like to thank the following specialists, companies, breeders and hobbyists for their advice and kindly letting us use their slides. We also thank all those we might have forgotten.

| | |
|---|---|
| A. Camoens | H.-G. Evers |
| H. Hieronimus | H. Nakano |
| Y. Muira | T. Tarpley |
| F. Teigler | N. Tomizana |
| F. Schäfer | H.-F. Schmidt-Knaatz |
| E. Schraml | U. Werner |

**Aquarium Glaser GmbH,**
for providing beautiful fish for our photographers from their weekly imports.

*amtra* - **Aquaristik GmbH,**
for providing furnished aquaria
and equipment for testing.

**Veterinary consultant:**
**Dr. med. vet. Markus Biffar,**
veterinarian, fish specialist

**Liability:**
All the information in this book has been recorded with due care and attention. The authors and the publishers will not accept liability for any inaccuracies.
By purchasing this book the owner explicitly accepts this disclaimer of liability.
All rights reserved. Except for private study, research or review no part of this publication may be reproduced, stored in any retrieval system or reproduced in any form by any means without the permission of the publishers.
Further useful tips about care and maintenance can be found every six weeks in **AQUALOG***news*, the unique newspaper for all friends of the hobby.
Read, for example, the latest breeding reports in the *news.* It is available in German or English and can be obtained at your local pet shop or subscribed to at the publisher. Order your free specimen copy!

AQUALOG: Special-Serie Ratgeber
Rodgau: A.C.S.
South American Freshwater Stingrays

South American Freshwater Stingrays
Richard A. Ross
ISBN 3-931702-87-1
(German edition: ISBN 3-931702-88-X)
NE: Ross, Richard

© **Copyright by:**  Verlag A.C.S. GmbH
Liebigstr. 1,
D-63110 Rodgau
Germany

**Author:**
Richard A. Ross
**Index and Organisation:**
Wolfgang Glaser
**Editor:**
Dipl. Biol. Frank Schäfer
**Cover Layout:**
Frank Schäfer

Lithographics: Frank Teigler/A.C.S.
Layout: Bettina Kirsch/A.C.S.
Druck: Westermann Druck Zwickau
Printed on EURO ART
100% chlorine free paper

Redaktionsanschrift:
Verlag A.C.S. GmbH
Liebigstraße 1
D-63110 Rodgau
Fax:        +49 (0) 6106 – 64 46 92
E-mail: acs@aqualog.de
http://www.aqualog.de

**PRINTED IN GERMANY**

Front Cover Photo and page 2/3: *Potamotrygon motoro* „Ornament"
(photo: E. Schraml, Archiv A.C.S.). Back Cover Photos: *P. motoro*, juv.
(photo: A. Camoens), *P. leopoldi* (photo: R. Ross), *P. yepezi* (photo: E. Schraml, Archiv A.C.S.).

# Contents

# Foreword

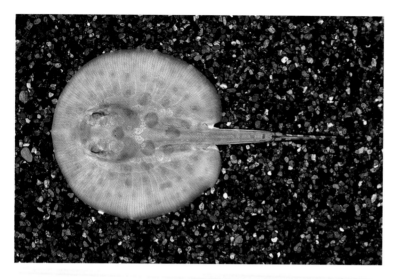

*Freshwater stingrays are often fantastically brightly coloured. This, together with their unusual shape, makes them much sought after. But all ray species grow very large and, more-over, make other special demands on their owner. photos: A.C.S. archives*

Wherever rays are exhibited, whether in a Zoological Garden or in a home aquarium, they are always the center of attraction. Simple yet seccessful, elegant and graceful, stingrays are among the most beautiful of all aquatic animals. Their unique shape and mode of swimming, their expressive "faces", and their compatibility with other fish species stimulategreat interest in the home aquarist. Unfortunately the existing aquarium literature on these fishes is sparse, the information available is often contradictory or incorrect. This guide by Dr. Richard Ross will fill this void in the aquarium literature. Dr. Ross is a Consultant in fish and reptiles to the Santa Barbara Zoo in California, and has studied these demanding and fascinating creatures for many years. In this guide, he provides all the information he has acquired, presented in a practical and easy-to-use form.

The stingray design represents over 50 millions years of successful evolution. The remarkable similarity between fossil marine stingrays and contemporary freshwater rays shows that their design has changed little over many million of years. Originating in shallow oceans and inland seas, these fish migrated into brackish and then fresh water to escape predators or find food, and now inhabit the river systems of South America, Africa and Asia. Although different thearies exist as to when and where these migrations occured, paleontologists agree that freshwater rays evolved from marine rays.

Unfortunately many species of freshwater stingrays are becoming endangered through destruction or degradation of their habitat. Logging of rainforest and mining destroys or contaminates the river systems upon which stingrays depend for survival. Moreover, as is often the case with venomous animals, there is little interest in protecting these fish. While stingrays are potentially dangerous, few people realizethat their feared sting is actually a defensive weapon and never used aggressively. It is therefore important for all people to be aware of the existance of these delicate and beautiful animals, and consequently to understand the need for protecting their habitat.

Although in recent years successful breeding of stingrays has increased, the majority of these breedings are fortuitous, and the most specimens offered for sale in the trade are wild-caught. The number of rays captured for the pet trade is relatively small, and probablydoes not create a threat to the survival of the species.

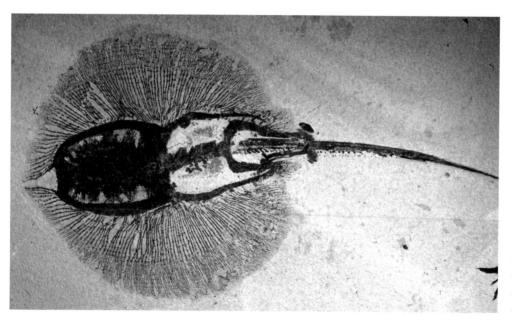

*Fossil of a stinray.*

Nontheless, the fact that specimens offered in the pet trade are wild-caught, imposes a clear responsibility on the aquarist who purchases them. A basic knowledge of their husbandry requirements is an unconditional prerequisite if stingrays are to be kept successfully, especially if the aquarist is interested in captive breeding. Dr. Ross provides the necessary husbandry information in this book. He also stresses that stingrays are suitable only for a minority of aquarists. Those aquarists

# Foreword

who are unwilling or unable to provide the large aquariums and filtration systems necessary, or are unwilling to exercise the necessary caution and safeguards inherent in keeping venomous animals should reconsider keeping these fish.

It is to the author's immense credit that he does not hesitate to describe his own negative experiences and failures with freshwater stingrays, and he is willing to identify areas where he has been unable to find solutions to problems in the husbandry of these fish. It is through continued efforts to resolve these husbandry problems that we will be able to improve our ability to successfully keep freshwater stingrays in captivity.

Personally, I always consider the main criterion in evaluating books to be the number of "eye-openers" and "Oh, I see" points that I discover when reading the book. In this case they were numerous. I believe this book should be compulsory reading for each and every aquarist who is considering keeping stingrays, whether it be zoological gardens and other institutions or the home aquarist. I am also quite sure that even "old hands" will find it highly beneficial reading.

Enjoy!

Frank Schäfer

*Above: Freshwater stingrays are ecologically very flexible and are often found in unexpected places, for example in fast-flowing stretches of river. Unfortunately they, like all the life in many South American ecosytems, are increasingly threatened by water pollution and environmental destruction. photo: U.Werner.*

*Below: Motoro type rays are regularly bred in the aquarium.*

## HISTORY AND DEVELOPMENT

### Evolution of South American Freshwater Stingrays

A longstanding hypothesis of freshwater stingray evolution was proposed by BROOKS, and suggests that before the Andes mountains uplifted, about 80 million years ago, marine rays of the Pacific Ocean had migrated into coastal areas of the Amazon and become adapted to brackish water. During that time, the Amazon flowed into the Pacific Ocean. As the Andes were formed, during the Cretaceous period, the Amazon reversed its flow and became an eastward-flowing river, gradually trapping the stingrays in fresh water. This theory was based on analysis of the parasites of freshwater and marine stingrays, and suggests that Potamotrygonid stingrays are closely related to marine rays of the genus *Urolophis*.

Using DNA sequencing, a new hypothesis has recently been proposed by LOVEJOY, which suggests that stingrays evolved more recently by incursions of marine rays from the Caribbean area into rivers draining into the Atlantic Ocean. This theory proposes that freshwater stingrays evolved more recently, about 20 million years ago during the Miocene era. The DNA analysis shows that South American freshwater stingrays are more closely related to marine rays of the genus *Himantura*.

Although it is not possible to know which theory of stingray evolution is correct, it is likely that freshwater rays evolved in some way or other from marine rays. Fossil stingrays from North America show that stingray anatomy has changed little in the past 50 million years. These fossil stingrays are presumed to be marine, and to have inhabited shallow inland seas in the area that is now Wyoming and Montana. Either to escape predators, or by chance migration into the mouths of rivers, marine rays gradually became adapted to brackish water, and finally to fresh water. Having lost the salt gland found in marine rays, freshwater rays are no longer able to eliminate salt from their blood, and cannot tolerate the marine environment.

### Stingray Taxonomy

In 1986 Ricardo ROSA re-assessed the taxonomy of freshwater stingrays. His taxonomy was based primarily on morphological and osteological studies of museum specimens, and cannot be easily applied to living specimens. Because freshwater stingrays are highly polymorphic, variations in patterns, as well as in physical structures such as spines and tail length, are common, and taxonomic criteria based on physical criteria are likely to be uncertain. Therefore, it is still difficult to assign scientific names to many specimens.

The word "morph" is used to describe different-looking specimens of the same species. In some cases morphs are con-

*A good example of polymorphism is provided by the species Potamotrygon henlei. On the lefthand side of the picture is a light morph specimen, with two individuals of the dark morph on the right.*

sistent, in that only a few exist of a given species, and they always have the same appearance. In other cases, a species may be so variable, or polymorphic, that many morphs exist and there is no consistency in their appearance. A good example of a highly polymorphic species is the common stingray, *Potamotrygon motoro*. This species is usually sold simply as the "motoro stingray". However, there are many morphs of *P. motoro*, and there is not much consistency in the variations. Some specimens have many small ocelli, while others have few large ocelli. Some specimens are dark, others are light. A relatively non-polymorphic species is the tiger ray. While there is an ontogenetic colour change that occurs during growth, there is very little variation in the adult colour and pattern. The only consistent variations are a dark and a lighter morph.

The absence of a consistent taxonomic determination plus a high degree of polymorphism makes the taxonomy of stingrays difficult, and creates problems in the ornamental fish trade. Many species, or morphs, have names used by the indigenous people in the region where the stingrays are found. Sometimes these names can be translated into English. Other names may be derived from indigenous native dialects. In many cases, morphs have been given names

that have no specific meaning, but have been accepted into common usage. The names used in this book are names used by the ornamental fish trade, as well as scientific names wherever the scientific name is not in question.

A detailed introduction to the taxonomy of the rays, together with an identification key, will be found in the AQUALOG identification catalogue "Freshwater Rays".

**Stingray Anatomy**

Stingrays are members of the elasmobranch class, a group of fish that includes sharks, marine and freshwater rays, and sawfish.

*Above: At first glance these rays are very similar. But if one looks more closely, then distinct differences in the pattern can be detected. Are these species or morphs? A question that can be very difficult to answer.*

*Below: In "tiger ray" species the juveniles (right) are differently coloured to adults, although the basic pattern is the same in both cases.*

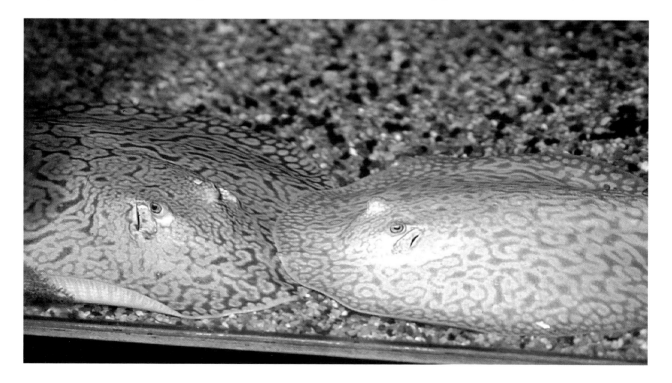

# History and Development
## Stingray Anatomy

Left: Close-up of a small-eyed ray (China ray), and to the right a large-eyed species (Potamotrygon histrix). In both cases the spiracle (spiraculum) right next to the eye is clearly visible.
right: A.C.S. archives

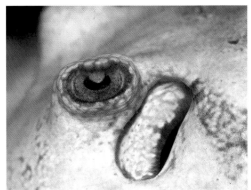

Elasmobranch fish are unique in many ways. They do not have scales; in the place of scales their skin has dermal denticles, giving it the texture of fine sandpaper.

The venomous sting or barb (see below) of the rays is also a modified denticle. As in all Elasmobranchs, the teeth are shed constantly, and are replaced by new ones throughout the life of the fish. As in the „normal" teeth in the mouth of the rays, the sting is shed about twice yearly, and is replaced by a new one. It is common to see stingrays with two and occasionally three stings. The largest sting, usually the one closest to the end of the tail, is the oldest, and will be the first to be shed.

Elasmobranchs do not have calcified bones; instead their skeleton is composed of cartilage. Stingrays have an accessory respiratory opening, the spiracle, which is an adaptation to living directly on or buried in the substrate. Scientists believe that the spiracle is a modified gill slit which, over time, has migrated to the dorsal surface of stingrays.

When the animal is resting on the river bottom, the gill slits may be on the sand or mud, and water cannot pass through them. The spiracle opens on the dorsal surface, or top, of the ray, directly behind the eyes, and allows the animal to breath when resting on the bottom.

Stingrays can be divided into two groups based on eye structure. The more commonly imported species have large, protruding eyes elevated above the body. The pupil is large and U-shaped. This elevated position allows the ray's eyes to protrude when the fish is otherwise completely buried in the substrate. This eye position seems to be adapted to allow good visibility. The second group, less commonly imported, has small, non-protruding eyes with a smaller, simpler, pupil. These rays probably have poor vision, and, in the wild, may remain buried in the substrate most of the time. They may also live in rivers where the visibility is poor, and hence good vision is not important.

Stingray eyes include a structure called the *operculum pupillare*, which controls the amount of light that enters the pupil. In bright light this structure expands to reduce the light entering the eye. In dim light it retracts to allow more light to enter.

The stingray's digestive system has evolved an unusual structure in the intestinal tract, the spiral valve. This structure increases the absorptive surface of the intestine by adding many layers or folds to the mucosa, or lining of the intestine. As food passes through the digestive tract, it passes through this spiral valve and thus the waste has a ribbon-like twisted appearance. The spiral valve is also found in sharks and other primitive fish.

In all ray species the gill opening (G) is on the underside of the body. This is the most important character distinguishing them from the sharks, in which the gill opening is sited on the side of the body.
M = mouth opening
N = nostril
photo: A.C.S. archives

N →
M →
G →

# Stingrays and Man
## How Dangerous are Stingrays?

### STINGRAYS AND MAN

#### How Dangerous are Stingrays?

The sting, spine, or barb, located midway along the tail, is a defensive weapon. Many specimens will have two, or even three spines. The sting is not used indiscriminately to attack humans, nor is it used to attack other fish. Nonetheless, people living in the areas where stingrays are found fear them. This is because their sting is extremely painful, and, additionally, medical attention or even simple first aid measures are often unavailable to people who have been stung.

There are two common ways people are stung. Adults or children may be stung while wading barefoot in the water, and children may be stung in the abdomen when diving into shallow water. Fishermen may also be stung by a stingray brought into the boat on a fishing line.

Because stingrays are widely feared, they are often indiscriminately killed. While it is understandable that rays are feared, it is unfortunate that they are killed, as they do not intentionally attack man, and injuries result from humans invading their territory. Like all animals that are potentially dangerous to man, they deserve respect and protection.

*Above: The intact spine(G) has a fleshy sheath. Stingrays may have one up to three spines. This differs individually and is not species-specific.        photo: F. Schäfer*

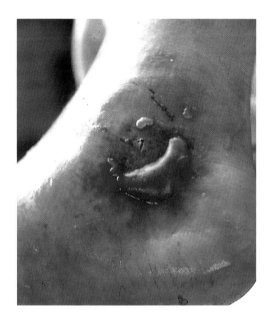

*Centre: A stingray-inflicted wound two days after the mishap. The wound took several weeks to heal, and the area was still numb six years after the event.*
*photo: Frank Warzel*

### THE SPINE AND VENOM

The stingray's spine is primarily a defensive weapon: we have rarely observed rays attempt to sting deliberately, even when

*Below: A number of detached stingray spines, such as are likely to be found in the aquarium over the course of time. One spine still carries the airline tubing used to sheathe it during transportation.*

**Anatomic Details of a Freshwater Stingray:**

G = Gill
K = Kidney
S = Stomach
B = Bowel
L = Liver
R = Rostral cartilage

# The Spine and its Venom
## First Aid for Stingray Envenomation

*A newly-imported tiger ray, both its poison spines still sheathed with airline tubing.*

netted or manipulated during treatment. Stingray envenomation from captive specimens is uncommon, and although individuals who have been stung report that the venom is extremely painful, none suffered any serious consequences. However, it is important to understand that toxicity of stingray venoms or toxins may vary between species, as is the case in many types of venomous animals. Although fatalities are not known to have occurred as a direct result of stingray envenomation, it is possible that while some species may have painful but harmless venom, others may have potentially fatal venom.

We have been unable to find studies performed specifically on freshwater stingray venom. It may be that there is a toxic chemical within the sting. It is also possible that the fleshy sheath surrounding the spine may have toxic qualities, or may be responsible for secondary infections. The primary risk appears to be from secondary infection from wound contamination.

### First Aid for Stingray Envenomation

The toxins, or venoms, of stingray spines appear to be protein molecules which can be temporarily inactivated by hot water. First aid for stings, therefore, consists of keeping the affected area immersed in hot water, or covered by a towel soaked in hot water. The water should be as hot as possible without causing burns. Usually this will alleviate the pain. Once first aid has been applied, medical advice should be obtained immediately. Remember: there are many species of stingrays, and little is known about the toxicity of individual species' venom. Although fatalities are not known to have occurred as a direct result of stings by stingrays, if you should be stung, you must seek medical help to avoid secondary infections or other complications.

### Points Worth Remembering about the Poison Spine

Stingrays may have from one to three spines present at one time. A fleshy sheath covers the spine. When the spine becomes embedded in an animal or a net, the sheath often tears away. Therefore, newly imported specimens often have an exposed spine. Once the sheath has been avulsed (torn away) from the spine, it will not regrow. As new spines develop, the oldest spine is shed. A spine is shed approximately two to three times per year. Discarded spines may be found at the bottom of the tank. These spines may have residual amounts of toxin, and should be handled with care. Envenomation has occurred from careless handling of dead rays, and also from specimens that have been kept frozen for long periods.

# Rays as Aquarium Fish
## The Spine in Freshly Imported Rays

## RAYS AS AQUARIUM FISH

### The Spine in Freshly Imported Rays

It is common practice for exporters to place a piece of air hose or other plastic tubing over the spine to prevent injuries to workers, as well as to prevent the spine from becoming caught in nets or perforating plastic shipping bags. If left on the spine, this tubing can create several problems: it can catch on wood or other objects in the tank; it twists the sting as the ray swims, putting stress on the tail. The additional weight and torque placed on the spine by the tubing can cause the spine to be torn free, leaving an open wound at the insertion site on the tail. When tubes are placed on the spines, they are often forced over the spine's protective tissue sheath, damaging the tissue. The damaged tissue is susceptible to infection, especially during holding periods where water quality and filtration are substandard. Purulent, necrotic, material is often found in pieces of tubing when they have been removed, or fallen off, indicating that infections were present.

Additionally, several specimens in our collection developed sepsis after the spine fell off prematurely as a result of the air hose. It is therefore highly recommended that these tubes be removed from the spine as soon as possible after specimens are received.

Because of the difficulty in removing the tubing, rays should not be placed in their permanent tank until the tubing has been removed. This can be done prior to removing the ray from the shipping bag, or while it is in the quarantine tank. If the ray is agitated and makes removal of the tubing difficult, it may be necessary to anaesthetize the ray with the fish anaesthetic tricaine methanesulphonate (brand names MS-222, Finquel).

These tubes are extremely difficult to remove from the spine, due to the spine's reverse teeth. However, they should always be removed, even if this requires anaesthetization of the specimen. Removal is best performed when the specimen has recently been received and is still in the shipping container. The easiest method of removing the tubing is to hold it at its end with forceps,

*As soon as the airline is removed the injuries caused by it may bleed profusely.*

*The fleshy sheath of the poison spine does not regenerate.*

*These poison spines were cut after they became entangled in the net during capture.*

while cutting off the top of the tubing with a razor knife or scalpel, starting from the end closest to the ray's body. Care must be taken to avoid injury, both to the ray and to the aquarist! When the top of the tubing has been cut away, the rest of it can be spread apart with forceps or other instrument, and removed.

After removing the tubing, the area around the spine should be examined for signs of infection or bleeding. If such signs are present, the ray should be put on a course of an antibiotic (by injection) and kept in an isolation tank until all signs of infection have disappeared. No less than three doses of antibiotic on alternate days should be given.

### Problems with Very Large Rays

Stingrays available in the pet trade are often significantly larger than other ornamental fish. While medium-sized rays less than 12 inches (30 cm) in diameter generally withstand shipping well, very large specimens are much more sensitive to the stresses of capture, handling, and shipping. Long flights, delays in making connections, and poor water quality are responsible for a significant mortality rate in any species of large fish and also in imported rays. Additionally, rays are stressed by being captured and held by natives, by being roughly handled during transport to exporters' facilities, and finally by being kept in inadequate conditions before being exported. Some specimens that reach the ornamental fish trade have been caught by fishermen on hooks. Once they arrive at the importer's facility, they may be kept for as little as one to two days, and then shipped again. When they finally reach the retail fish store or ultimate destination, they may have been subjected to two or three weeks of substandard conditions.

## Problems with the Importation of Very Small Rays

An additional stress caused by shipping, especially for very small stingrays, is lack of food. Fish generally are not fed for one to two days before shipping to reduce excretion of waste in transit. This is no problem for large, healthy specimens. However, very young specimens have little reserves. When this period of starvation is extended by long transit times, the stress becomes more severe. It is therefore important to be able to examine stingrays for signs of stress and poor condition.

## Appearance of Healthy Rays

Rays in good health should have clear skin, and a velvety appearance. Light-coloured patches on the skin are likely to be areas where fungal infections are beginning to develop. An overall cloudiness or milky discoloration is also a sign of disease, especially fungal infections. Injuries to the skin are potential sites for infections to develop: fungal infections are rarely primary infections; instead they tend to develop secondarily where bacterial infections have begun and dead tissue exists. However, once the dead tissue becomes infected with fungus, the fungus will then invade healthy tissue and continue to spread. Fungal infections caused by the freshwater fungus *Saprolegnia* are often seen on the tail, especially where a piece of air tubing has been placed over the spine (see page 13), or at the tip where minor injuries may occur during handling. These infections appear as small cottonwool-like tufts. Fungal infections of this nature are generally not serious, and usually disappear when the specimen is kept in a properly maintained aquarium.

Fish that are severely but briefly stressed often do not show abnormal physical signs for 7 to 10 days. For this reason the initial period after shipping can be critical. Rays that appear healthy with no abnormal signs may initially do well, only to deteriorate days later. Whenever possible, newly received fish should be kept in a quarantine or isolation tank during this period, at least until they have been feeding well for several days. Early signs of poor health are listlessness, cessation of feeding, failure to begin feeding, and fin curl.

*Healthy rays are lively, and their skin exhibits no cloudiness. The pelvic bones should not be visible in well-fed individuals.*
*photo: A.C.S. archives*

# Rays as Aquarium Fish
## Appearance of Stressed Rays

*The "death curl" (this is a mantilla ray).*
*Right, just beginning; below, far advanced.*

Rays with any of these signs should be kept in tanks with excellent water quality, good filtration, and aeration, and should immediately be started on an antibiotic treatment program.

**Appearance of Stressed Rays**

When examining stingrays for potential purchase, the most important sign to look for is curling of the disc, or margin of the fin. This is sometimes known as the "death curl". A healthy ray always keeps the disc margin flat to the substrate, except when actively moving about the tank. A ray that consistently holds the edges of the fin elevated or curled upwards slightly while at rest will almost inevitably die. The cause of this problem is not known; however, it is an extremely reliable sign. There are two possible exceptions to this: a ray may be resting in a current of water that causes the fin to be elevated, and rays in good condition at rest will sometimes slowly undulate the fin, or disc, on either side of the tail. The physiological cause of this problem is unknown: a healthy ray should always rest with the disc margin flat or curled slightly inward, as if gripping the substrate. This is probably a normal reflex posture, and loss of this reflex may indicate loss of central nervous system (brain) function. This suggests that fin curl is a sign that the fish has been badly stressed for some time.

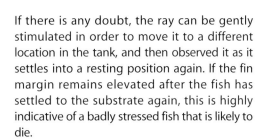

If there is any doubt, the ray can be gently stimulated in order to move it to a different location in the tank, and then observed it as it settles into a resting position again. If the fin margin remains elevated after the fish has settled to the substrate again, this is highly indicative of a badly stressed fish that is likely to die.

In the early stages of this problem the trailing edge of the disc margin will be affected first, on either side of the tail. When the problem spreads around the disc towards the front, death will soon occur. Such specimens should never be purchased unless the aquarist is willing to risk almost certain loss of the specimen. The aquarist should always be aware of this sign, and be prepared to identify it at its earliest stage. When it occurs in an acclimated specimen or long-term captive it is an ominous sign, indicating an overlooked problem.

# Rays as Aquarium Fish
## Evaluation of Nutritional Status

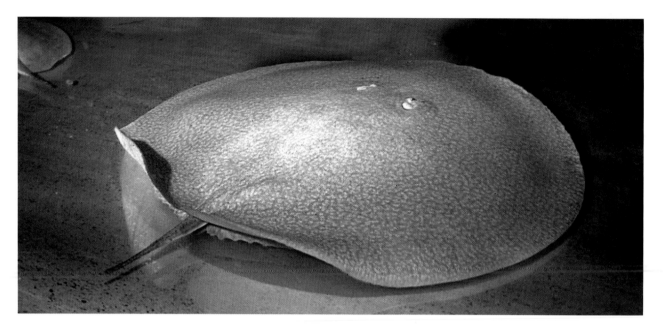

*Coly ray exhibiting normal behaviour, with no fin curl.*

It is important to note that some species of rays will slowly undulate the caudal margin of the disc when at rest. Small-eyed rays commonly exhibit this behaviour, and it does not have the same significance as fin curl.

Other signs of poor health or disease are a cloudy or milky film covering the body, rapid breathing while at rest, open sores on the body, red or bloody sores on the underside of the fish, and areas of fungal infection on the skin. While these signs may indicate disease or stress, they are not necessarily indicative of imminent death; curling of the disc margin is a far more serious sign.

### Evaluation of Nutritional Status

Stingrays should also be examined for weight loss. The tail and pelvic bones are the areas where weight loss will be most apparent. The pelvic bones are located on the ray's dorsal, or upper body, on either side of the tail, where the tail joins the body. When visible, they appear as small tent-like elevations of the skin. The pelvic bones should not be visible on a ray in good nutritional condition. Similarly, the tail should be full and thick, with no bony structure visible through the skin. Rays kept without feeding for long periods, either by exporters or retail shops, may show these signs of weight loss.

Although a recently imported ray may have lost weight due to having spent several weeks in transit without being fed, once acclimated to captivity a healthy specimen should begin feeding and regain lost weight fairly quickly. When in doubt, a specimen in a shop can be offered food: an acclimated stingray, in good health and kept in suitable conditions, will almost never refuse food.

A ray in good health but showing signs of weight loss is likely to thrive once in a supportive environment, and should readily regain lost weight. Such specimens should be maintained in an isolation tank if possible to eliminate competition from tankmates for food. Specimens with visible pelvic bones must be very heavily fed in order to re-establish normal weight.

Stingrays are very active fish, and have a high metabolic rate. Feedings should be given two or three times daily: many weeks may be necessary to re-establish normal body weight in malnourished specimens.

Once malnourished specimens have been placed in a communal aquarium, they should be observed closely to be certain that they are competing successfully for food. It is particularly important to avoid overfeeding when acclimating newly acquired rays in a small quarantine tank, as live foods remaining in the tank can add significantly to the nitrate level.

# Rays as Aquarium Fish
## Quarantine and Acclimatisation

*A badly emaciated ray. The individual in the lower picture also shows the ominous signs of serious weight loss, in that the triangular pelvic bones on either side of the tail are clearly visible.*

### Quarantine and Acclimatisation

Whenever possible, new rays should routinely be kept in isolation tanks while being acclimated. When body weight is adequate, two weeks of acclimatisation and isolation is a good guideline. Although a healthy specimen may be ready to begin feeding in a day or two, the constant activity of large tank with many fish may delay or prevent a newly received specimen, even one in good health, from becoming acclimated. Newly acquired specimens may take a while to accept the unfamiliar foods offered in captivity; acclimated specimens search constantly and aggressively for food, leaving little for a new specimen to eat. Additionally, there is a risk of introducing infection or parasites into the tank if a newly acquired specimen is placed directly into a communal tank.

It is common practice in public aquaria as well as in importers' facilities to treat all newly acquired specimens with a broad-spectrum antibiotic and conditioning chemicals, or other products added directly to the water in order to suppress or eliminate incubating diseases. (For treatment of specific diseases see page 35 ff) While this is generally not a harmful practice, the dosages for these medications are arbitrary, and the absorption rate and effective activity of these dissolved medications are extremely

unpredictable. Freshwater fish do not drink water; therefore, drugs added to the water will not be ingested. Beneficial effect from dissolved antibiotics comes from two sources: the drugs will come into direct contact with the external surface of the fish where infections may be present, and some antibiotics such as the nitrofurantoin drugs may be absorbed through the gills of the fish.

Drugs commonly used for this purpose include nitrofurazone, sulfa drugs, tetracycline, and multiple drug and chemical combinations used in the exotic fish trade to alleviate stress and infections.

Some of the chemicals found in these

# Rays as Aquarium Fish
## Quarantine and Acclimatisation

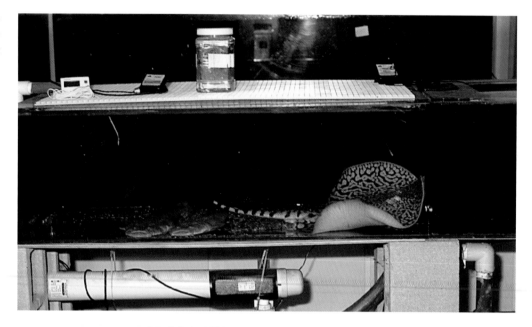

combination products may have no benefit whatsoever. For these reasons, whenever an obvious infection is present, single drugs are preferred over multiple drug combinations. In addition, injectable medications are superior to medications dissolved in the water.

Medications that may be useful when dissolved in water are nitrofurazone, chloramphenicol, and metronidazole. Chloramphenicol can only be obtained by prescription. Metronidazole is used primarily for specific parasitic infestations.

Because of the difficulty in seeing and removing fish lice (*Argulus*), it is wise to treat all new specimens for this ectoparasite by adding Dimilin to the water for ten days. Fish lice are easily overlooked, and can remain on a stingray for months before beginning a reproductive cycle. Outbreaks of *Argulus* have occurred in our collection up to one year after the most recent addition of fish.

Occasionally specimens that appear to be in good health may refuse food and eventually die. Unfortunately such unexplained deaths are puzzling for the aquarist, and causes can rarely be found. The most likely explanation for these unexplained deaths is exposure to some form of extreme stress during capture and transport. Specimens may be held in poor conditions for extended periods by the natives who capture them for the ornamental fish trade. Specimens are often transported

in plastic bags or small buckets by boat. Failure to provide fresh water can result in accumulation of nitrogenous wastes in the water. Toxicity from elevated levels of ammonia, a nitrogenous waste, may cause permanent kidney damage, which produces no visible signs in fish. Bags or buckets containing fish may be be exposed to the sun for many hours. Exposure to high temperatures can cause invisible organ or tissue damage. Once renal failure occurs, death is inevitable, but may not occur for several weeks.

A second cause of unexplained death may be permanent neurological damage from elevated ammonia or low oxygen levels in the water. Where water quality is poor, the dissolved oxygen level may be low and ammonia high. Hypoxia, or low oxygen (hypoxia is a low oxygen level in the fish, as opposed to the water), and elevated ammonia both can cause brain damage or generalized tissue death. High ammonia levels in the water may also contribute to hypoxia by causing gill damage.

These conditions may not cause immediate death, but may cause irreversible brain or other organ damage eventually resulting in death weeks later.

# Aquarium Design and How to Keep Rays
## Aquarium ornamentation

**AQUARIUM DESIGN
AND HOW TO KEEP RAYS**

Only the smallest of stingray specimens are suitable for a small (about 100 cm / 39 inches in length and 40 cm / 16 inches in width) or community tank with other fish species. Newborn specimens, often called "teacup rays", are imported at 6 to 8 cm / 2,5 - 3 inches in width. These small stingrays can easily be kept in small aquaria. However, once acclimated, they will grow rapidly, and soon outgrow a small aquarium. Additionally, the majority of the more interesting species of stingrays are imported at larger sizes, or adult sizes, and these specimens cannot easily be kept in a community aquarium.

Therefore, the aquarist who keeps freshwater stingrays should choose or construct an aquarium designed primarily for stingrays' requirements. Other fish species can, of course, live in such aquaria, but the shape will be more suitable for the rays as they grow.

When fully grown, most freshwater stingrays can reach at least 50 cm /20 inches in diameter, and sometimes over one metre / 39 inches.  For this reason stingrays should never be purchased for aquariums of less than 200L, as they will soon outgrow small aquaria.

The rate of growth for stingrays depends on how much and how often they are fed, as well as on water quality. When kept in a well-maintained aquarium with optimal food supply, a ray will reach adult size in about three to four years.

It may not be possible to purchase a prefabricated aquarium ideally suited for stingrays, as even the largest of stingrays does not require water more than two feet deep. A custom-made aquarium can be constructed with a greater surface area and viewing area than would be available in prefabricated aquariums of the same volume. Our aquaria for large rays are 3 metres /10 feet in length, but only 1.75m / 70 inches deep. Stingrays that are 45cm / 18 inches or more in width should have an aquarium at least 120 cm / 4 feet in length and 60 cm / 2 feet in width.

**Aquarium ornamentation**

Aquarium decoration will depend primarily on the size of the specimens. In a communal tank, with small stingrays, traditional ornaments such as driftwood, rocks, live or plastic plants, etc, are suitable. However, with larger specimens live plants will not survive for long. The rays will constantly turn over the substrate looking for food, and live plants will soon be uprooted and destroyed. In addition equipment in the tank, such as plastic lift-tubes, glass heaters, or submerged filters, may be dislodged or broken by larger specimens. Even powerhead pumps held in place by suction cups can be knocked loose by rays looking for food. In our collection it is not uncommon for stingrays to move large rocks weighing several pounds, or to move large pieces of driftwood or even other fish while searching for some small morsel of food.

Rocks or pieces or driftwood with sharp edges should be avoided: stingrays can become injured or cut by sharp edges. Submerged heaters also represent a problem for stingrays. In our experience, the rays do not always sense the excessive heat created by a heater. Two stingrays in our collection were badly burned from resting on heaters. Therefore, whenever possible the aquarium heater should be placed either in the sump of a wet-dry filter, or covered by rocks, gravel or other tank ornaments to avoid injuries. But never bury a standard aquarium heater completely! It will  overheat and crack.

Although rays do not generally jump out of the water, aquaria should always be covered. Glass tanks generally have straight sides with either a small internal lip or no lip at all. Rays will routinely slide up the sides of tanks when exploring their environment or trying to catch feeder goldfish; glass tanks without a cover are therefore very risky, as the rays can easily slide up and over the top of the glass. A ray can also slide up the side of a tank and into the lighting reflector. In the United States, acrylic aquaria generally are constructed with a large lip which is adequate to prevent rays from escaping.

However, on two occasions rays in our collection have jumped out of acrylic tanks.

In the first instance the ray actually managed to jump through a small gap of less than three inches between the cover and the lip of the tank: it may have become startled or frightened during the night. In the second, the ray, a 40 cm / 16 inch specimen, jumped out of a quarantine tank with a 10 cm /4 inch lip. We therefore recommend that a cover be used for all stingray aquaria, but especially for aquaria without an internal lip.

### Water Parameters

Water chemistry and quality is determined by a few specific parameters. These are:

- hardness and conductivity
- pH
- nitrates and nitrites
- dissolved oxygen (DO)

Stingrays, like many freshwater fish, are tolerant of a wide range of conditions. Many freshwater systems, such as lakes, rivers, and ponds, are much less stable than marine environments. By comparison with marine environments, changes in pH, temperature, hardness and dissolved oxygen occur relatively rapidly and regularly, so fish must be able to tolerate such changes to survive. Although stingrays are fairly forgiving of changes in water parameters, the aquarist must still pay rigorous attention to maintaining appropriate water chemistry and good water quality, because changes will occur regardless of how well an aquarium is managed.

### Hardness and Conductivity

It is generally true that freshwater stingrays prefer soft water, below 200 microsiemens when measured as conductivity, or 7°dGH when measured as total hardness. Ceja rays seem especially sensitive to elevated hardness when freshly imported. New specimens show a twitching motion of the disc when swimming or resting, as if irritated by something in the water. They also do not begin feeding. A level of below 150 microsiemens is often necessary for newly imported specimens. After about one year, most specimens, including ceja-type rays, seem to adjust to harder water. They no longer show the twitching movements, and

feed regularly. However, this group of rays does not thrive in captivity generally, and it is still recommended that hardness be kept at a very low level.

### The pH Value

While freshwater rays are indigenous to soft acid water, the majority of species will tolerate a wide range of pH once they have been acclimated. Newly acquired specimens should be kept in a range 6.5 to 7.0, at least for several weeks. We have observed new specimens that were listless and refused to feed suddenly become active and begin feeding when the pH was lowered from a range of 7.3-7.4 to 6.25.

Once acclimated, stingrays do well in water that ranges from a pH of 6.00 to 6.75. Most species will tolerate a pH range of 5.0 to 8.0, if changes occur gradually. While the ability to tolerate a wide range of water conditions is fortunate and desirable, experience shows that more ideal conditions are required for captive breeding. Captive breeding is a more accurate measurement of water require-ments than is longevity in captivity. In captive breeding situations it has been found necessary to maintain pH at a much more steady level and to avoid rapid changes. In addition, when very low pH levels occur in the wild this is due to natural processes rather than inadequate aquarium maintenance or addition of chemicals.

### Nitrite and Nitrate Sensitivity

Stingrays are also said to be highly sensitive to elevated levels of nitrite and nitrate. Early husbandry literature suggests that weekly water changes of 25% or more are necessary to maintain adequate water quality. Although our experience is that rays are, in general, no more sensitive to these nitrogenous wastes than other freshwater fish, we have observed individual variation in tolerance to nitrate among different stingray species. The majority of stingray species thrive at nitrate levels ranging from 100 to 200mg/L. At levels of 300mg/L, some species in our collection have stopped feeding, while other species showed no ill effects. When exposed to levels of 350 to 400mg/L for one week, most species showed loss of appetite,

# Aquarium Design and How to Keep Rays
## Water Parameters

but when the nitrate level was reduced to below 300, they returned to normal, suggesting that no permanent damage occurred to the fish during that time.

Symptoms of nitrate toxicity in some species under experimental conditions have occurred at nitrate levels of 400mg/L or more. These specimens stopped feeding, and became very inactive, only moving when touched with an instrument. Some specimens developed seizure-like activity, characterized by twitching or shaking movements. When these specimens were moved into water of perfect quality, the symptoms disappeared very slowly. These rays did not begin feeding for over three weeks, and the seizure-like activity disappeared after this time.

### Water Changes

There is a common belief that stingrays require more water changes than other tropical fish. When kept in a well-maintained aquarium, this is not necessary. With good filtration and water management, our experience is that stingrays thrive under the same regime as other tropical fish. A 20% water change every two to four weeks is adequate, depending on the bio-mass, or numbers and size of fish. Actual size and frequency of water changes required can be established best by regular monitoring of nitrate levels. There is, however, a major difference between stingrays and most other tropical fish.

The experience of most aquarists is that their fish either are purchased at adult size, or grow very little before reaching maturity. By contrast every species of stingray that we are aware of, with the exception of the black-tailed antenna rays, will grow to at least 50 cm / 20 inches, and many will reach adult size at one metre / 39 inches. The bio-mass of an aquarium with stingrays is thus, in a sense, increasing constantly. When keeping sting-rays, the aquarist must never become com-placent about a routine water management schedule. Water parameter testing should always be a part of aquarium maintenance. It is only through regular testing for nitrate and pH, and hardness or conductivity, that sting-rays can be successfully kept.

### Salt

There is a general belief that freshwater stingrays will not tolerate salt (sodium chloride - NaCl); other aquarists believe that adding salt is essential for maintaining the health of rays in captivity. The former opinion is probably based on the lack of salt-excreting glands in freshwater rays; the origin of the latter opinion is unclear, but may be based on the common practice of exporters of adding salt to the water. Collectors and exporters of tropical fish in Latin America traditionally add large quantities of salt, NaCl, to the water in their holding facilities. We measured the water at some of these facilities in Iquitos, Peru, and found that whereas incoming water from the municipal water supply measured 30 to 40 microsiemens conductivity (compared to zero in the nearby river), water in stock tanks measured from 1500 to > 2000 (off the scale). This appeared to be due entirely to the addition of large quantities of NaCl, as evidenced by the pots of salt located at the ends of the rows of aquariums in many facilities. We initially suspected that this might be responsible for the moderate mortality rate of rays when shipped into the US, but exporters insisted that the high salt content was necessary in order to avoid heavy losses.

The use of salt as a preventative against stress or shock in shipped specimens is another aspect of salt metabolism in freshwater rays. When stressed, marine elasmobranchs may undergo osmotic shock characterized by rapid sodium loss. Although this has not been documented in fresh water rays, it may be explain why the addition of NaCl by exporters is effective in preventing deaths. The duration of exposure to high salt concentrations is an important factor in assessing tolerance, and fish generally do not spend more than several days to a week in exporters' facilities. A short-term exposure to high salt may be less toxic than long term exposure at lower levels.

A possible explanation of the role of salt in preventing stress is the difference in salt content between fresh water and fish blood. Because the blood of fish contains a much higher level of NaCl than fresh water, there is an relative imbalance between water and the blood vessels of the fish's gills, requiring a significant energy expenditure to maintain the high serum sodium chloride level. The addition of salt to the water reduces this difference, thus lowering the required energy expenditure and reducing osmotic stress on the fish. Moreover reducing the ionic gradient of NaCl between the ray's blood and the surrounding water reduces the loss of salt caused by stress. For these reasons, salt has important therapeutic value in reducing the physiological effects of stress. The addition of salt to the water of rays that are sick, as well as those that have recently been shipped and therefore almost certainly stressed, is recommended.

Salt is also highly effective in eliminating fungus from aquaria. Although it may not cure fungal infections, it will reduce the likelihood of spread. Table salt usually contains iodine, and it is not known if this is safe for all fish. Therefore rock salt is preferable. A safe dosage is one tablespoon per gallon / 4 L. This corresponds to about 2% to 2.5% salinity.

*Large but peaceful predators, such as the tiger catfish (Merodontus tigrinus) shown here, are usually good tankmates for rays.*

### Water Temperature

Water temperature for rays should be in the range of 75-80F / 24-26°C. Rays seem comfortable at temperatures of 80-82F / 27-28°C, but we have lost some specimens when the water temperature exceeded 86F / 30°C. As with nitrate, there seems to be some variation between species as regards temperature tolerance. Brief exposures to cold temperature (60-65F / 16-18°C), such as occur during shipping in cold weather, do not appear to cause permanent harm or illness. However, chronic exposure to temperatures below 70-72F / 21-22°C may cause anorexia and illness. Tiger rays are particularly sensitive to temperature: this species will not thrive unless maintained within a temperature range of 78-82F / 25,5-28°C.

## COMPATIBILITY OF STINGRAYS WITH OTHER FISH

### General Considerations

Although stingrays are not aggressive fish, keeping them in a communal aquarium can

# Compatibility of Stingrays with Other Fish
## General Considerations

present problems. Rays generally show little or no interest in other fish. As rays grow, however, any small fish may eventually become prey for them. Stingrays grow in proportion to how much they are fed, and most imported species can grow to very large size. However, like most aquarium fish, if they are fed small amounts regularly, their growth rate will be slow. Other than the concern for eating smaller fish, stingrays are tranquil fish.

Keeping more than one specimen in the same tank generally does not present problems, and stingrays will ignore other fish that are too large to eat.

While many tropical fish establish territories which they defend vigorously, stingrays rarely interact aggressively and do not seem to be territorial in nature. Different species likewise do not interact aggressively, nor does significant difference in the size of specimens kept together create problems. Except for species requiring special conditions (see below), numbers of rays of

different species and sizes may be kept together without difficulty as long as there is adequate food.

When keeping numbers of rays together, the aquarist should provide food at least twice daily, and observe each specimen during feeding to be certain that all are obtaining sufficient food. It is easy to underestimate the amount of food necessary for stingrays.

*Above: In general different ray species are very tolerant of each other.*

*Below: The stripe-like marking on the edge of the body disc of this specimen is attributable to an old injury.*

## Compatibility of Stingrays with Other Fish
### Aggressive Behaviour

*Above: The so-called "topping", a relatively harmless type of aggressive behaviour in rays.*

*Below: Tiger rays sometimes chase one other.*

Aquarists are accustomed to purchasing fish of adult size, as well as fish being small when full grown, so their food requirements do not change much. To the contrary, even small stingrays, which are larger than most common aquarium fish, are still juveniles, and require much more food, as they are growing rapidly.

Once acclimated, a stingray should never have visible pelvic bones. Whenever this occurs, it is a clear indication of inadequate feeding, and the feedings should immediately be increased.

### Aggressive Behaviour

Although uncommon, aggressive behaviour can occasionally occur between stingrays. Adult males may bite each other (there do exists reports that fertile males, especially of the relative aggressive species of the motoro-group, even killed each other), and males will bite females during courtship. Occasional bites of this nature are harmless, but severe injuries have been known to occur, especially during courtship. Such injuries usually occur around the disc margin, or along the backbone, and are characterized by abrasions or frayed areas. Even severe injuries to the disc margin generally heal quickly if the ray is in good health.

Wild-caught specimens often have irregularities of their pattern at the disc margin,

# Compatibility of Stingrays with Other Fish
## Rays and Suckermouth Catfishes

Although suckermouth catfishes of the genus Panaque (this is P. nigrolineatus) are actually strict vegetarians, under certain circumstances they may seriously injure rays.

indicating areas where healed injuries of this type are present. These healed injuries may appear as short stripes or other pattern irregularities.

It should also be remembered that, as in any animal species, individual variations in "personality" occur. Some individuals are naturally more aggressive than others: like any captive collection of animals, stingrays should always be observed for signs of injuries or aggresive behaviour. Aggressive behaviour between rays can sometimes result in dominance behaviour, which can in turn cause a subordinate specimen to stop feeding and act listlessly, often hiding in one corner of the aquarium. In the wild a subordinate specimen can escape a dominant individual; in the aquarium this is impossible. As a result a subordinate specimen may be repeatedly injured and will eventually stop feeding and die. In such cases there may not be severe injuries, but careful observation will show that the dominant ray is constantly biting or chasing the subordinate one. In addition to injuries around the disc margin, abrasions or bite marks may appear on the dorsal surface of the ray, especially along the backbone. When this behaviour is observed, either the dominant or the subordinate specimen must be removed, or the latter will eventually die. Two specimens in our collection were killed by such aggressive behaviour.

A common and harmless form of mild aggression called "topping" often occurs in

rays. This is characterized by one ray completely covering another, or sitting on top of the other ray. Sometimes the upper ray will simply cover the eyes of the ray underneath. This behaviour rarely includes biting, and tends to be harmless. Stingrays will perform this behaviour on other fish species as well as other rays. We have observed rays to cover plecostomus species that have been irritating them.

### Rays and Suckermouth Catfishes

Rays in aquaria are rarely injured by other fish. However, some plecostomus will annoy stingrays by chewing on them. It is not known if the plecostomus actually consume the slime coat or skin of the stingrays, or if this is a form of aggressive behaviour. It can,

however, be a serious problem. A persistent plecostomus can cause serious injury and ultimately death of rays if not removed. Typical injuries are scrapes or abrasions along the back. Often the careful aquarist will observe the plecostomus sitting on the ray's back, only to be dislodged repeatedly by the unhappy stingray.

## SUBSTRATES

### General

Some controversy exists regarding the best substrates for stingrays. In the wild freshwater stingrays are often found in areas where the river bottoms are composed primarily of mud, silt, or extremely fine sand. These types of material are not suitable for the average aquarium for several reasons. Firstly, the fine particles are too easily disturbed, and, since they do not settle quickly, are eventually sucked into filters. Secondly, they are likely to create anaerobic conditions if areas of compacting occur.

As stingrays lack scales, their skin is very delicate. The dermal denticles present on the dorsal surface may provide some protection, but the ventral surface lacks even dermal denticles, and is therefore even more sensitive. Substrates composed of particles

*Above: The damage to this ray was also caused by a suckermouth catfish.*

*Below: On the other hand, the scars on this ray date back to old "love bites" during the mating season.*

*Once they are settled in, rays only occasionally bury themselves in the substrate.*

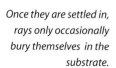

# Substrates
## What Type of Substrate is Suitable

*This ray can smell food and is leaving its resting-place.*

that are sharp or abrasive will damage the rays' skin. This ultimately results in fungal or bacterial infections which are often fatal, therefore a substrate should be chosen carefully in order to avoid this problem.

Unfortunately there is little consistency in the types of gravels and sands supplied for aquaria. Smooth gravels of any kind are suitable. Genuine non-silica sands are probably suitable. However, when in doubt do not use sand: although sands seem to work satisfactorily in some areas of the US, other areas experience difficulty with locally available sand and this doubtless applies equally in other countries too.

### What Type of Substrate is Suitable

It is extremely difficult to obtain accurate information regarding the silica content of sands from rockyards where these materials are bought in bulk: it has been our experience that such information is unreliable, and we have lost stingrays on sand substrates that were described as "low silica". The precise factor accounting for these differences is not yet known.

A major problem in selecting a substrate is the fact that the terms "sand" and "gravel" are used for materials that have tremendous variation in their composition.

Regional differences are one source of the problem: sands and gravels from one part of the country may bear little resemblance to those from another area. The term "aquarium gravel" does not necessarily indicate a consistent product.

River sands tend to be smoother than ocean sands, and desert sands differ as well. Additionally, it is often difficult to get precise information about the content and composition of sands and gravels from rockyards or building supply companies that sell them. The silica content and sharpness of the grains are the primary concerns. Fine silica sands or any sharp sands may abrade the rays' skin (see below), providing a site for infection to develop.

*Healthy rays are always hungry. This Potamotrygon leopoldi is investigating the corners of its aquarium in the hope of finding something to eat.*

## Maintenance without Substrate

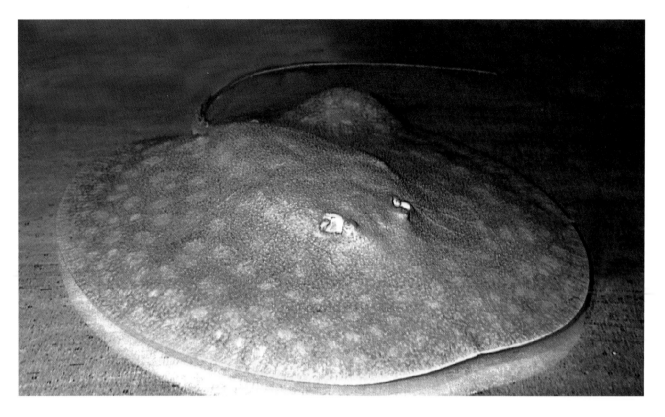

### Maintenance without Substrate

Several alternatives exist. Stingrays will actually do well in bare-bottomed tanks, although they are often uncomfortable for some time before becoming acclimated to these conditions. Stingrays utilize their pectoral fins for moving slowly across the substrate; without a substrate they will be unable to gain traction, and slip when trying to "walk" on their pelvic fins. Eventually, however, they seem to adjust to this. Bare-bottomed aquaria are especially suitable for quarantine tanks, as it is easier to tell if food has been eaten.

### Maintenance with Substrate

Stingrays often bury themselves in the substrate, especially when startled. Occasionally rays will bury themselves while inactive and lie with only their eyes protruding. Rays also like to turn up the substrate by blowing water into it, looking for bits of food or hidden worms.

Substrates should not be too deep when used in aquarium systems without under gravel filters, as anaerobic areas may develop in areas where the substrate has become compacted. In addition, uneaten food can accumulate in thick layers of gravel. Normally very active, stingrays will constantly blow into the gravel looking for food, and this will keep the substrate relatively clean and free of debris if it is not more than one to 6 cm / one and half inches deep. Furthermore it is wise to clean the substrate on a regular basis, perhaps once weekly, with a gravel cleaner or "hydro-vac" to be certain that there are no areas of accumulating debris.

As rays become fully acclimated they spend less and less time buried in the substrate, and eventually spend most of their time looking for food or exploring their tank.

With regard to substrates in general, the most important factor seems to be the behaviour of the specimen rather than the actual material. Delicate taxa, such as the ceja-type rays, china rays, and tiger rays do not do well on substrates that are problem-free for other taxa. This is probably due to their tendency to bury themselves in the substrate regularly, eventually resulting in abrasions in the skin. Other taxa which are less shy in captivity rarely bury themselves, and therefore do well in various substrates. We have used coarse or medium aquarium gravel successfully with many ray species.

# Feeding Stingrays
## What Stingrays Eat

Also suitable are the more ornamental gravels composed of smooth dark-colored pebbles.

Aquarists from other areas in the US report using local sands and gravels without problems: when uncertain as to which substrate to use, graded aquarium gravels may be the best choice, as they seem to be fairly consistent in their composition regardless of the region.

## FEEDING STINGRAYS

### What Stingrays Eat

Stingrays will eat a wide variety of foods. Maintaining a varied diet is extremely important in captive animals, as monotonous diets create a risk of nutritional deficiencies. Stingrays are very active, and should be fed at least once a day, preferably twice or even three times daily. The daily diet can be varied in order to create some environmental enrichment as well as a balanced diet for the rays. The following are suitable food items:

- feeder goldfish or other small fish
- pieces of crushed fresh fish
- ghost shrimp, small crayfish or grass shrimp
- blackworms or other tubificid worms (rays sometimes prefer blackworms to tubifex worms)
- chopped night crawlers (large earthworms)
- redworms or other commercially raised worms
- pieces of raw shrimp
- krill (not floating: rays cannot eat floating foods!)

First foods for newly acquired rays should be blackworms respectively tubifex or very small pieces of fresh fish: these foods seem to be the most readily accepted, and are small enough to be inadvertently ingested either by mouth or through the spiracle, thereby giving the ray an opportunity to taste these possibly unfamiliar foods by chance. Foods that have been used for very small specimens, such as the "teacup rays", are small insect larvae such as mosquito larvae, small shrimp known as "ghost shrimp" or "glass shrimp", and live brine shrimp, as

well as blackworms. Small chitinous foods such as these shrimp species provide less nutritional value than do soft-bodied foods, so should not be used as the sole food items.

*A ray that has been accustomed to feeding from forceps taking an earthworm.*

The best way to be certain that a new stingray is feeding is to watch the spiracles as the ray passes over food on the bottom of the tank. If it is eating the spiracles will open and close rapidly, or flutter, as the food is ingested and water is passed from the mouth and out of the spiracles. Once a newly acquired ray is observed to be readily feeding on blackworms, finely chopped night crawlers can be introduced in small quantities. Once recognized as food, these will be readily eaten by nearly all stingrays. Other types of food can be experimented with later.

*Small-eyed rays will eat only live fish. The photo shows a china ray that has captured a feeder goldfish.*

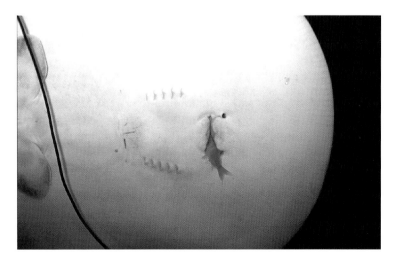

# Feeding Stingrays
## What Stingrays Eat

*Rays blow into the sand, mouth protruded, in order to stir up and capture small food organisms or morsels of food.*

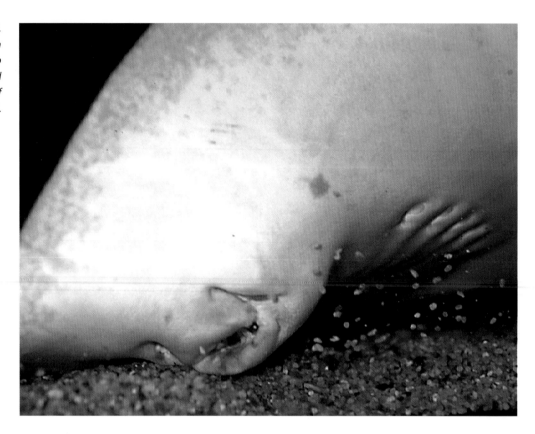

*Rays search for food in the sand, and also like to rest there. The correct choice of substrate is thus immensely important.*

# Feeding Stingrays
## What Stingrays Eat

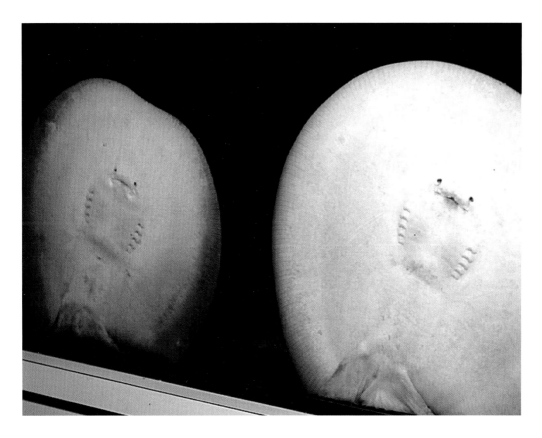

The small-eyed rays (left a Manzana ray, right a China ray), like to cling to the vertical glass panes of their aquarium and wait there for food.

This ray is inquisitively investigating a root for previously overlooked morsels of food.

## Training Rays to Hand Feed

### Live Foods

Live foods, including blackworms or tubifex worms, can be fed in quantities adequate to allow a small amount to be left in the tank to allow the rays to browse later. However, when cleaning the substrate note whether a significant number of living worms are present: blackworms and tubifex worms will colonize the substrate if not eaten, and add to the nitrogenous waste production in the aquarium. Stingrays live on the bottom of the aquarium most of the time, and if there is not adequate circulation or turbulence, the water quality at the substrate level may deteriorate if the substrate becomes colonized by live worms.

### Other Foodstuffs

Chopped earthworms, redworms or nightcrawlers, and any non-live, non-aquatic foods should be fed in smaller quantities in order to avoid overlooked food decomposing in the tank. Keep in mind that stingrays have relatively small mouths: a 40 cm / 10-inch ray may have a mouth 2-3 cm / 1/2 to 3/4 inch wide, so chopped food items must be small enough to be easily eaten. If a ray ingests a piece of food and repeatedly spits it out and ingests it again, this usually indicates that the particle size is too large. Some ray species such as antenna rays have even smaller mouths relative to their size.

There are reports that some specimens like to feed on plants. These fish even ate small pieces of cucumber. In the Frankfurt Zoo aquarium (Germany), where motoro-rays are bred regulary, they are fed with a gelatine-bound food that contains also vegetarian particles.

Once acclimated, rays often develop techniques for eating larger foods. For example, newly imported rays may have difficulty in consuming even small chopped pieces of nightcrawlers. Eventually, however, they learn to eat an entire worm by sucking it into their oral cavity without chewing. In addition newly acquired rays often ignore feeder goldfish, but they quickly learn to chase down and consume these "feeders", even learning where they tend to hide in the tank.

Stingrays may learn to eat other unfamiliar foods such as brine shrimp, pellet foods, or other commercially prepared foods. While there is probably no harm in offering these foods to rays, it is best to utilize fresh live foods as the dietary staple.

Occasionally a well acclimated specimen will fail to gain weight, even though you are offering enough food. Several things may cause this problem. The most likely possibility is that it is not competing efficiently for food against other fish in the aquarium. Alternatively, it may have a parasitic infestation

### Training Rays to Hand Feed

Specimens in our collection occasionally seem not to learn where foods can be found and are always in the wrong part of the tank during feeding times. In these cases it is helpful to "hand-feed" such specimens. By this I do not mean feeding with your hands: although some aquarists do this with sting rays I do not recommend it, because of the possibility of accidents. Instead, hand feeding of specimens should be performed with long forceps or a similar instrument. Stingrays generally avoid metal objects: they appear to be frightened by metal. However because they can sense metal, they will quickly learn that when there is a metal object in the aquarium, food is being offered. In this way you can teach your stingray to feed directly from forceps, and selectively feed it more food.

Simply hold a night crawler (or a piece of night crawler) in the forceps, and hold the worm in the aquarium so that the ray can touch it with its fin. It should eat it immediately. After a few feedings in this manner, allow the forceps to touch the ray while it is eating the worm. It will quickly learn to associate the forceps with feeding, and soon you will find that the ray will pounce on the forceps as soon as it touches them, eagerly looking for food.

### How Often to Feed

The key to having well-fed stingrays is providing plenty of food. Unlike most fish that swim quietly between feeds, stingrays

# Health and Disease
## The behaviour of healthy and unhealthy stingrays

search constantly for food, looking under and around tank ornaments, moving driftwood, rocks, filters, and even other fish! This high activity level translates to a high metabolic rate, which means that while searching for food rays continuously burn energy. If they use up energy looking for food, but do not find food, they are losing weight. To compensate for this loss of energy it is essential to provide adequate food.

This cannot be over-emphasized: hobbyists sometimes feed their rays three times weekly, thinking that this is adequate. Our specimens are fed at least twice, and usually three times, daily: in spite of this frequent feeding our specimens are still constantly looking for food between feeds!

### Feeder Goldfish

When feeding significant quantities of live feeder goldfish, it is wise to add vitamin B1 to the feeder supply. Goldfish are known to contain the enzyme thiaminase in their tissue which destroys thiamin, or vitamin B1, and this vitamin must be replenished. It is our practice to add one 50mg tablet to each 2.000L / 500 gallons of water every two weeks. The tablets are added directly to the sump of the wet-dry filter; alternatively the tablets can be added directly to the tank.

### HEALTH AND DISEASE

### The behaviour of
### healthy and unhealthy stingrays

Once acclimated, rays should be constantly observed for any indications of health problems. Stingrays exhibit both obvious and subtle signs of health, which can readily be observed.

Most species, if received in good condition, will begin feeding in about 2 to 3 days. Some specimens may take as long as one to two weeks, especially the small-eyed rays and tiger rays. Rays are normally active and inquisitive, and should soon begin exploring a tank and searching for food. Rays that remain quiet for more than a few days, or refuse food after this time, should be closely monitored for signs of illness, injury or stress.

Rays that appear in good health but do not begin feeding should be kept in an isolation tank until feeding has become regular. Shy or stressed specimens may starve in the midst of abundant food if kept in a tank with many busy, active, fish.

Healthy stingrays always eagerly accept food, and between feeds are almost always searching for food in the tank. Stingrays will rarely refuse food when offered, even if they have recently been fed. Thus the first sign of a health problem in rays is often refusal of food. If a ray refuses food even once, it should be examined carefully for signs of disease. Often the first noticeable abnormality is an area of fungal infection on the skin (excluding the tail, where such infections are more common). Other signs of health problems are rapid breathing, decrease in general activity, and remaining buried under the substrate for long periods. If no signs of ill health are observed in a specimen that refuses food, water quality parameters should be checked. Other factors that may be responsible for loss of appetite are subtle interactions with other rays or other fish species, such as dominance behaviour related to sex or size differences, or aggressive behaviour by other kinds of fish. This can explain why one ray will refuse food when others in the tank act normally.

Healthy stingrays demonstrate typical patterns of activity. Rays will spend most of the time searching the tank for food. They browse around the tank, blowing water into the substrate to search for leftover blackworms or tubifex worms, or search under driftwood, rocks, and other tank ornaments for food. From time to time they will rest by burying themselves in the substrate for a few moments, with only their eyes showing. Sometimes they rest with a few grains of gravel on their back. Usually they will soon surface to look for food again. While resting on top of the substrate, healthy rays often slowly undulate the tail end of their fin, or disc. This is especially common among china rays and ceja rays. Ceja rays often prefer to adhere to the side of the tank, waiting for feeder fish which they trap against the side of the tank. Additionally, most rays will swim actively along the sides of the tank, surfacing above the water line

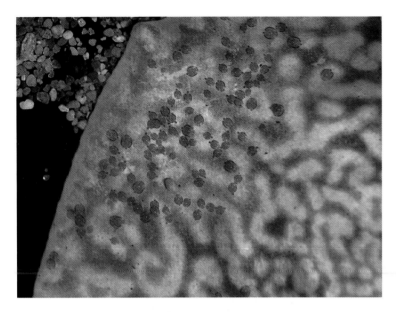

from time to time. This is normal inquisitive, or exploratory, behaviour. However, healthy rays rarely spend much time free-swimming in the tank. A ray that spends most of its time swimming freely in the water rather than along the substrate may be exhibiting the effects of stress.

**Diseases and Parasites**

Stingrays in captivity do not seem susceptible to the common diseases of tropical fish. Diseases such as "ick" (*Ichthyophthirius multifiliis*), are rarely if ever seen. Occasionally newly imported specimens may carry *Argulus*, an arthropod commonly known as the fish louse.

**Argulus**

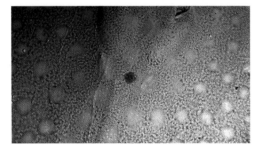

*Although the odd parasite may escape the aquarist's notice (above right), heavy infestations of Argulus such as that shown above left can no longer be overlooked.*

These ectoparasites appear as small brown spots, about 2-3mm in diameter. They may at first appear to be circular spots on the skin of the ray, and are more readily seen in light-coloured specimens. When gently touched, however, they will quickly move across the ray's skin. Stingrays are also sometimes infested with a large and colourful species of *Argulus* that were even thought to be the juveniles of the rays!

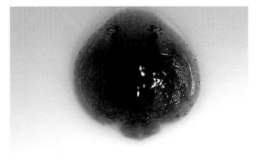

*Close-up of a fish louse (Argulus).*

*Argulus* are usually seen in small numbers, two or three at a time on the fish. Although small numbers of *Argulus* are not harmful, they can eventually multiply and thus be more harmful. *Argulus* feed from rays by penetrating the ray's skin with an organ called the style. The parasite then sucks fluid from the ray's body through this organ.

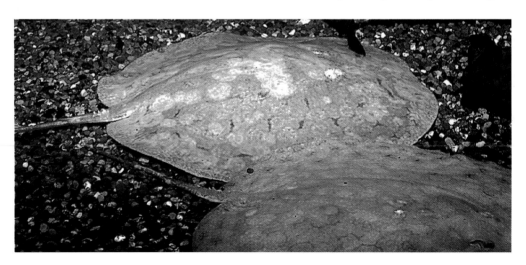

*The light area on the back of this Ceja ray is indicative of fungus attack.*

# Health and Disease
## Argulus

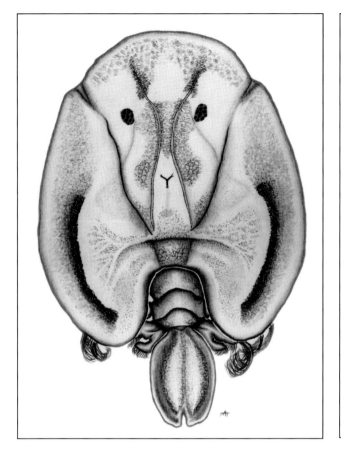

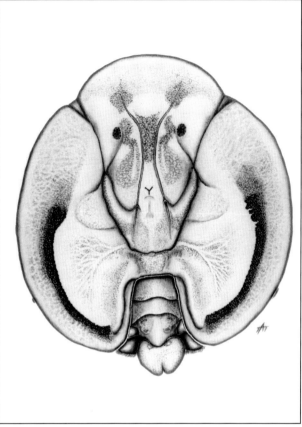

When these parasites are present, the penetrating wounds can become secondarily infected and eventually become fatal. When only a few lice are present it is not too difficult to remove them by hand. If the lice are on the dorsal surface of the ray, they can most easily be removed with forceps, by pinching the parasite and removing it. When on the ventral surface, removal is trickier: turning the ray over is very difficult, and it is easier to pinch the parasite through the net with the fingers in order to remove it. Heavier infestations can be treated with the medication Dimilin, a newly available drug which inhibits chitin formation in crustaceans. This medication is quite safe for fish, as it is highly specific in its action: it affects only the formation of the chitin exoskeleton of the parasites, and has no effect on the fish. Dimilin is sold under the brand name Anchors Away, as it is also used for anchor worm in fish. Simply follow the instructions on the bottle. Another drug often used for *Argulus* is Dylox: this product is toxic to rays, and should not be used.

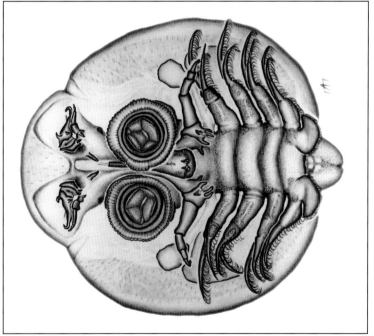

*The unique detailed markings of an as yet undetermined Argulus species, collected from a South American freshwater stingray. Above left, dorsal view of the male; above right, the female, also in dorsal view; below, ventral view of the female.*
*Drawings: Tom Tarpley.*
*(By kind permission of the Southeast Aquatic Research Institute, Tennessee.)*

## Fungal Infections

*Fungal infection of the tip of the tail, as seen in the young ray on the right, is generally harmless, but should nevertheless always be treated.*

### Fungal infections

Fungal infections are the commonest diseases of freshwater stingrays. Fungal infections may occur secondarily to bacterial infections resulting from injuries, or they may occur in badly stressed fish with reduced immunity. Damaged tissue becomes infected with bacteria, and this becomes the site for the fungal infection to develop. The fungus can then spread to previously healthy tissue.

Fungal infections are commonly seen on the tail and sting of freshly imported specimens, perhaps secondary to injuries from capture and handling. It is common practice at importers' facilities to add various antibiotics to the water supply: these drugs may help to suppress or cure bacterial infections, but since antibiotics do not affect fungi, it is still common to see such fungal infections in specimens received from importers.

Small fungal infections at the tip of the sting or tail generally are not dangerous, and will heal spontaneously once the ray is in an aquarium with good water quality. Also, fungal infections generally do not spread to healthy fish. Nonetheless it is wise to isolate

specimens with fungus infections. The fungus can gently be removed with a forceps. It will then be possible to see if there is an underlying injury.

In any case, salt (NaCl) should be added to the water (0.1-0.2% solution), for this is useful against the fungal infection and, as already shown (p. 23), reduces the physiological effects of stress in the stingrays.

### Fin Rot and Other Bacterial Infections

Stingrays do not generally develop fin rot like other tropical fish. However, when kept in poor conditions during capture and shipping, or if kept in an aquarium with poor water quality, they may develop reddened sores on the ventral surface. These sores may result from being kept on inappropriate substrates, such as concrete pens or from poor water quality at exporters' facilities, or even from injuries from the stings of other rays if kept in crowded conditions. Bacterial infections can easily develop in such injuries, and therefore antibiotic treatment is appropriate whenever they appear. If found in a newly purchased specimen, these sores are likely to have been caused by shipping and handling, and should be treated during the quarantine period. However, if you suddenly observe a lesion of this nature in a specimen in your aquarium, it is an ominous sign that there is a serious problem with aquarium maintenance, as it suggests an internal bacterial infection.

### Medical Treatment

Medications available for diseases of stingrays include the general types of antibiotics and antifungal agents in use for ornamental tropical fish. Many products available for treating fish diseases are combination drugs which may include dyes such as methylene blue in addition to antibiotics such as nitrofurazone and furazolidone. While it is sometimes helpful to use combination drugs, it is also confusing, as it becomes impossible to know with certainty which of the drugs in the combination is effective. This "shotgun" approach to treating diseases of fish is commonly used, but should be avoided when possible.

*This tiger ray is suffering from fin-rot, as can be seen from the reddish coloration of the edge of the body disc.*

# Health and Disease
## Medical Treatment

Other medications used for fish include acriflavin, sulfa drugs, and tetracycline. These medications are added to the water as either a preventive for newly received fish, or treatment when a disease is suspected.

There are several problems incurred when using drugs in this manner. Firstly, charcoal filters tend to remove them rapidly from the water. Secondly, they can destroy bacterial filter beds. Thirdly, since freshwater fish do not drink, their rate of consumption by the fish is highly unpredictable. Fourthly, the dosage level is extremely unreliable. Fifthly, the duration of activity of dissolved drugs is also unpredictable. As a result of these problems, injectable treatment is the preferred method of antibiotic treatment. When access to injectable antibiotics is unavailable, the most useful antibiotic is nitrofurazone. This medication does not damage bacterial filters, and is more readily absorbed by fish when added to the water. The dosage is 250mg per 100L / 25 gallons. The treatment must be repeated every 3 to 4 days, as the drug breaks down in water. When treating fish by adding antibiotics to the water, it is necessary to do a 50% water change between treatments.

### Intolerance of Medications

Marine elasmobranchs are known to be very sensitive to a number of common fish medications. Although we do not yet know if freshwater stingrays are also sensitive to these medications, it is wise to avoid using them. Three examples are malachite green, a drug widely used to treat fungus infections, copper-containing medications, used to treat external parasites, and sulfa drugs. Ivermectin, a medication used to treat intestinal parasites is known to be toxic to both marine and freshwater stingrays. We have used sulfa drugs dissolved in the water (but not in injectable form) without any noticeable side effects on the fish. Since there is not much experience with medications for freshwater stingrays, always use new medications with caution. Reducing the dosage by 50% is one way to try new medications. We have used enrofloxacin (Baytril) and ceftazidime (Fortaz) by injection to treat bacterial infections secondary to air tubing injuries of the tail as well as fin rot. The dosage of

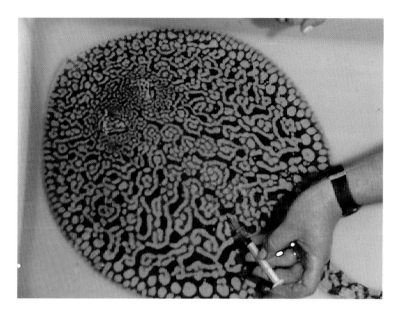

enrofloxacin is 0.25mg/kg every two days. The dosage for ceftazidime is 10mg/kg every two days. Injectable antibiotics generally must be obtained through a veterinarian. These antibiotics must be given by injection: they cannot be used by adding them to the aquarium water.

*Injections should be given only by qualified veterinarians! A second person should always be present to keep the ray's spine under control with a net.*

### Administering Injectable Drugs

Rays requiring drug injections should be netted and held immediately below the surface of the water. When removed from the water, rays will become panicky and thrash about, making it difficult to give the injection, as well as risking entanglement of the spine in the net. Therefore the process is facilitated if the spiracles are submerged. If two people are available, the ray's body can be supported from below the net with one hand, while the injection is being given with the other hand. The second person can hold the net.

For larger specimens too big to net and bring to the surface, the injection can be given under water. This requires some skill and caution, as the veterinarian must hold the loaded syringe under water, and corner the ray in the aquarium. The needle must be rapidly inserted into the muscle and the drug injected quickly, as the ray will usually pull away as soon as it feels the needle. This technique is not for beginners!

Whenever giving injections to stingrays, it is wise to use a net or other device to prevent being stung. Stingrays are surprisingly tole-

# Reproduction and Breeding
## Sex Determination

rant to handling and injections, but nonetheless it would not be unreasonable to expect a ray to react defensively when stabbed by a sharp object! An assistant can place the net or other baffle between the tail and the hand holding the syringe, so that if the ray attempts to sting, its tail will hit the baffle.

The site for injections should be slightly to the right or left of the spine, or backbone, about 2/3 of the way between the eye and the base of the tail. The needle should be inserted at a low angle to the ray's body rather than perpendicular to the body. The needle should be inserted about $1/2$ cm through the skin into the muscle.

*Care should be taken to avoid being within range of the sting when giving injections.*

### REPRODUCTION AND BREEDING

### Sex Determination

Stingrays, like other elasmobranchs, reproduce by internal fertilization. Male rays have claspers, which are modified pelvic fins, located on either side of the tail. The claspers are utilized to transfer sperm to the cloaca of the female during copulation. Claspers are present at birth, and thus sex can readily be determined even in very small or newborn specimens. However, until rays are mature, the claspers are small, and may be difficult to see without examining the ventral surface of a young specimen. This is most easily done when the ray is swimming against the side of the aquarium. For breeding purposes, it is necessary to differentiate between claspers of immature males and mature specimens. Claspers of mature males are easily visible, and protrude well beyond the edge of the disc. They appear as rolled layers of tissue. By comparison, claspers of immature males are small, simple, and do not protrude as far past the edge of the disc.

When considering captive breeding, it is important to remember that some species may be easily bred in captivity, while others may be very difficult. Species that are easily bred can create a false sense of achievement: data accumulated by breeding an easily bred species are not necessarily useful in breeding other species. An important factor in captive breeding is the age and size necessary to reach sexual maturity.

*Breeding pair with young. A sight to make the breeder's heart beat faster. In general adult rays are completely indifferent to juveniles, but nevertheless the young should be reared under controlled conditions away from their parents. An exception can be made in very large aquaria. In the Frankfurt Zoo Aquarium (Germany) it has been found that the young grow better and faster when left with the parents than separted brothers and sisters. photo: Y. Muira*

# Reproduction and Breeding
## Reproductive Husbandry

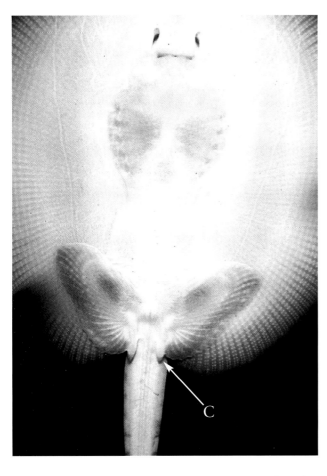

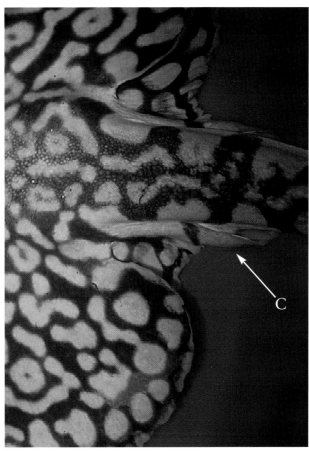

Some species, such as the otorongo group, antenna rays, and tiger rays do not reach sexual maturity until they attain a disc size of nearly 0.5 metres/ 20 inches. Other species, such as the motoro group and the black rays, will reach sexual maturity, based on the development of claspers in males, at a disc diameter of 30cm / 12 inches. For this reason these species are more easily bred in captivity than those reaching maturity at a larger size. Since large specimens are not often imported, it is rare that sexually mature specimens of many species will reach captivity.

There is no simple method to determine when females are mature. All freshwater rays are believed to bear live young. In known cases of captive breeding the gestation period has been about 3 months, although it is believed that in the wild gestation takes up to six months. Litter size has ranged from one to twelve in captivity.

Gravid, or pregnant, females can be identified by the symmetrical swelling on the dorsal surface at the base of the tail. The uterus islocated in this area, and enlarges visibly during gestation.

### Reproductive Husbandry

With rare exceptions, reproduction in fresh-water stingrays has been achieved only by chance. Even in those cases captive breeding has been restricted to few species, primarily those that are commonly imported. Captive breedings by hobbyists in most cases have been with *Potamotrygon motoro*.

As regards zoos and public aquaria, species bred in captivity include *P. magdalenae* (Belle Isle Aquarium), *P. leopoldi* (Aquarium of the Americas), and *P. motoro* (Exotarium Frank-furt). CAMOENS (pers. comm.) has worked extensively with three species (*Potamotrygon motoro, P. leopoldi, P. histrix*) and has collec-ted data on captive breeding for these species. While it is likely that captive breeding requirements differ from species to species, CAMOENS' data can serve as a basis for captive breeding.

*In young males the claspers (C) are still quite small and can be seen only from below. At the approach of sexual maturity they become long, easily visible from above, and spirally incurved. Females do not have claspers, so rays are easily sexed.*

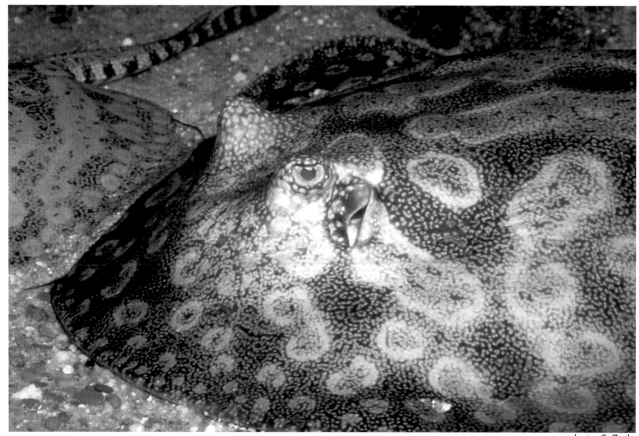

photo: G. Zurlo

photo: G. Zurlo

# Impressions
## Fascinating Freshwater Stingrays

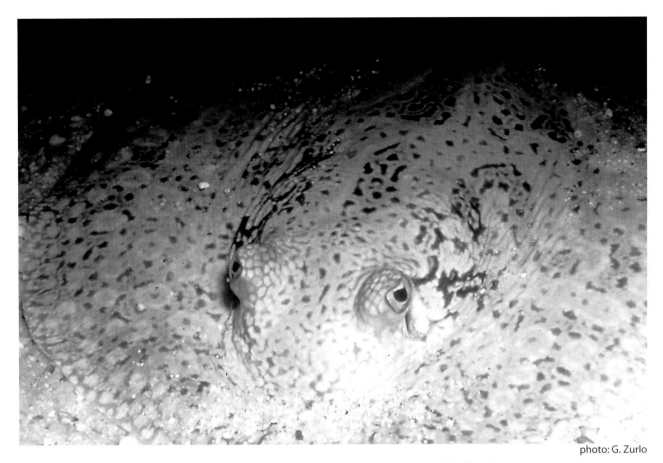

photo: G. Zurlo

photo: G. Zurlo

# Reproduction and Breeding
## Selection of Breeding Stock

*Unfortunately two rays of opposite sex do not automatically constitute a breeding pair. It appears that individuals of the same morph are more inclined to breed together than conspecifics which, however, belong to different morphs.*

### Selection of Specimens

Young specimens have proven to be more easily bred than specimens that were mature when imported. Acclimation of young specimens is often easier, and eventual adaptation to frequent contact with humans is more likely to occur. Specimens imported as adults are often frightened by aquarists' presence around aquariums, and this will interfere with reproductive behaviour. CAMOENS found that in similar aquarium circumstances, captive-raised adult specimens would reproduce when wild-caught adults would not.

CAMOENS also found that, in his experience, selecting the same morphs, or variants, within a species was important for success in breeding. He noted that specimens of the same

*In the course of their pregnancy gravid female rays develop a dorsal swelling*
*photo: Y. Muira*

# Reproduction and Breeding
## Courtship and Breeding Behaviour

"morph group" were more compatible than were different morphs of the same species. When he received juveniles (10 - 12 cm / 4 to 5 inches in disc diameter), these three species of rays required 3 to 5 years to reach sexual maturity. At sexual maturity, males were 25–30 cm / 10 to 12 inches in diameter and females were 35–45 cm / 14 to 18 inches.

### Special Feeding Requirements for Breeding

Routine maintainance feeding schedules are generally inadequate for captive breeding. Specimens that are part of a breeding program should be fed more food, and a greater variety of food if possible. CAMOENS fed shrimps, snails, guppies, tadpoles, crayfish, oysters, clams, krill, bloodworms, earthworms, worm pellets, tetra bits, crickets, and pieces of fresh fish including salmon, bass, or whiting.

Instead of keeping to a standard feeding schedule, different foods were offered in moderate quantities throughout the day. Foods were also dipped in a multi-vitamin powder.

The behaviour of specimens is a good guide to adequacy of feeding. If stingrays are constantly and aggressively searching for food, feeding should be increased. When rays' behaviour is dictated by hunger, reproduction is unlikely to occur.

### Water Quality Parameters

As with feeding regimes, water parameter guidelines for routine maintenance are not adequate for captive breeding. Most importantly, water parameters in general should not fluctuate significantly from day to day. Although most species of stingrays are able to tolerate such changes in water parameters, it is likely that in the wild, where conditions are relatively stable from day to day, changes occur over longer periods. CAMOENS found that stable water conditions were important for captive breeding. Because of the increased feedings necessary for breeding, the filtration system must be especially efficient to eliminate nitrogenous wastes.

Although CAMOENS attempted to duplicate the natural environment with branches, floating and submerged plants and other ornamentation, in many cases rays would breed in aquariums with no ornaments or gravel.

### Courtship and Breeding Behaviour

Early courtship may occur as long as two years before successful breeding occurs. This may be due to the female being unreceptive or not yet sexually mature. Early courtship behavior typically is characterized by the male pursuing and biting the female. Bites usually are around the disc margin, not on the back. Although small bites are most common, large pieces can be bitten off by the male. Serious injuries can occur during courtship, and occasional deaths of females have been reported.

In the wild, unreceptive females can find cover or flee; in the confines of an aquarium, unreceptive females are susceptible to constant attacks from aggressive males. If the aquarist notes that severe injuries are occurring, the female should be removed.

When the female is receptive, courtship can last two or three weeks. During copulation one of the two claspers is inserted into the cloaca of the female. Copulation takes place for approximately three minutes. As the clasper is withdrawn, the water may be clouded with sperm that is released. Both males and females resume normal foraging behaviour within minutes after copulation.

Once a female becomes gravid, her appetite increases so more food should be offered. CAMOENS estimated that food intake doubles for gravid females. Other than increased food intake, no change in behaviour was noted.
Water quality for gravid females is especially important. The gestation period is approximately three months. During that time sudden changes in pH, temperature, or levels of nitrogenous compounds (ammonia, nitrite, nitrate) can cause abortion. CAMOENS found that temperatures over 90 F / 32°C caused the female to abort, while temperatures as low as 70 F / 21°C had no effect.

Gravid females develop a swelling on the dorsal surface, surrounding the base of the tail. As parturition approaches, CAMOENS noted females becoming more active. Litter size varies from 1 to 6, and increases with size and age of the female. The young are often born with an intact yolk sac, which is absorbed in two or three days. No maternal care has been observed and no aggressive behaviour towards the young by adults was noted. Reports of young rays being eaten by adults may stem from inadequate food being provided for the latter.

### Newborn and Juvenile Stingrays

Special attention must be given to both juvenile and newborn stingrays regarding feeding. Firstly, these rays can only be offered the smallest of foods, which means blackworms, tubifex worms, or very small pieces of fresh fish. The mouth size of these small rays will be only a few millimetres, and therefore they will be unable to eat larger foods. Secondly, newborn or juvenile rays should be kept in aquaria with only a small amount of substrate, or in bare-bottomed tanks. They will not be strong enough to turn over gravel while foraging for food, so there is a risk that uneaten worms will colonize the gravel, adding to the nitrate load in the aquarium. When keeping small rays over gravel, the substrate should be turned over regularly to be sure that uneaten worms are not accumulating.

### Translocating Stingrays

Because individual rays commonly need to be placed together and subsequently separated during attempts to breed them, it is appropriate to mention here in some detail the special problems associated with the handling of stingrays.

Netting and moving stingrays is more difficult than with other fish for two reasons: first, rays are venomous, and second, the barb or spine readily catches in the meshes of most nets. The easiest method of translocating stingrays is to guide the specimen into a plastic shipping bag and raise it out of the water. As the bag is raised, most of the water can be drained from the bag. This method causes little stress or trauma to the ray. However, the spine of a large stingray can easily slash through even a thick plastic bag, so it is always important to avoid frightening a ray, and to make transfers as quickly as possible.

When a ray has to be captured for treatment, it is usually necessary to use a net. In this case a fine-meshed net must be used. This reduces (but does not eliminate) the risk of catching the spine in the mesh of the net. Chasing the ray around the tank should be avoided: rays are not agile swimmers and can usually be gently guided into the net. Once caught they can be raised to the surface for treatment: it is best not to remove the ray from the water entirely, as this may cause it to panic and thrash around in the net, risking entanglement of the spine. The ray should be held so that the spiracles are one or two cm / 1/2-3/4 inch below the water's surface. Once the specimen has been netted and raised to the surface, it is sometimes helpful to allow it to rest quietly for a minute or two, allowing it to become calm. The treatment is then more easily accomplished.

If the spine becomes caught in the net, it is sometimes possible to free it by gently pushing it backwards towards the ray's body to attempt to release the webbing from the reverse teeth of the spine. If this fails, as it usually will, it is best to cut the entangled tip of the spine free. As this is often necessary, it is wise to have a good quality, heavy duty scissors readily available while netting rays. Cutting the tip of the spine does not injure the ray. When the spine becomes caught, the fleshy sheath does not penetrate the net. This means that the tip of the spine is exposed and easily visible. Usually only the tip of the spine becomes caught in the net, so that cutting off 0.5 cm / 0.25 inches or at most 1cm / 0.5 inches will release the ray. The net should be raised to just below the surface of the water, and the spine should be cut as close as possible to the inside of the net.

If it is not possible to cut the spine free in this manner, a piece of the net can be cut away to release the ray. Never try to pull the net free, as this will only entangle it further. When a ray feels itself restrained by the net, it will swim away vigorously, which will enmesh the spine in the net more tightly, so the net should be cut away as quickly as possible, leaving a small piece attached to the spine. Do not remove the ray from the water while doing this, if possible, as this will cause the animal to be more frightened, making the procedure more difficult. Remember that stingrays are timid fish: the more quickly the net can be separated from the spine, the less they will be frightened. The piece of net will not bother the ray, and will fall off when the spine is shed.

Forcefully pulling on the net may cause the entire spine to be torn from the tail, leaving an open wound, which must be watched for signs of infection. Usually this will heal spontaneously. The fleshy sheath and spine will regrow in about 6 months.

## STINGRAY SPECIES GROUPS

### Large-eyed Rays and Small-eyed Rays

Stingrays can generally be divided into two groups based on eye size (see also photos, p. 10), the "small-eyed" and the "large-eyed" rays. Large-eyed rays have large, elevated eyes which protrude when the ray lies buried beneath the substrate. The pupil is large and U-shaped. Small-eyed rays have non-elevated small eyes with a round pupil. Although the differences in taxonomy of these groups may not be clear, the difference in the husbandry requirements of these rays is very important.

Large-eyed stingrays, the group which includes the majority of rays imported in the pet trade, are more vigorous and hardy than the small-eyed rays. The large-eyed group includes the otorongos, *Potamotrygon motoro* morphs, the black rays, *P. histrix* and *P. reticulatus*. These rays are generally aggressive feeders that constantly search the aquarium for food, foraging in the substrate or beneath tank ornaments. They will tolerate more varied water conditions, including harder water and higher nitrate levels.

The small-eyed rays include the ceja and manzana rays, the coly and china rays, and the antenna rays. Small-eyed rays are more delicate: they cannot tolerate nitrate levels over about 200 mg/l. They prefer soft water, although the antenna rays tolerate the same

hardness as large-eyed rays. The china, coly, ceja, and manzana rays will eat only live fish; the antenna rays will eat worms, and shrimp, but only the largest specimens over 25 cm / 10 inches will eat fish. It is especially important to keep small or young specimens of the antenna rays in bare-bottomed tanks or tanks with very little substrate. Small specimens of antenna rays are unable to move substrate to forage for food, and can starve while worms colonize the gravel.

### SMALL-EYED RAYS

This group includes the china rays, coly rays, the antenna rays, and the ceja-type rays (ceja and manzana rays). They are all more difficult to keep than the large-eyed rays. Some, like the ceja, china, and coly rays, are specialized feeders. Antenna rays, while accepting similar foods as other rays, are more delicate in captivity, and will not eat as wide a range of foods. All prefer soft, slightly acid water. They seem to be more sensitive to elevated nitrate levels than other species.

Ceja rays are found in Peru, and manzana rays, extremely similar in appearance, are from Brazil. These two rays are morphs of the same species, *Paratrygon* (formerly: *Disceus*) *aiereba*. The manzana ray does not have the "eyebrow" markings from which the ceja ray derives its name (see below, P.49). Both rays lack the terminal papilla typical of all other South American rays. Instead, the anterior edge of their disc is indented, or cardioid (heart-shaped) in shape.

### Antenna Rays

There are two types of antenna rays. The common antenna ray reaches a large size, up to one metre / 39 inches, and has an extremely elongated, delicate, tail. An intact tail will be three to four times as long as the disc diameter. Antenna rays have smaller mouths than most rays, and therefore feed primarily on blackworms or tubifex worms. Small specimens, under about 25 cm / 10 inches, are generally unable to eat even small pieces of chopped nightcrawlers. Finely chopped redworms and small shrimp may be eaten in addition to blackworms. Larger specimens will eat finely chopped nightcrawlers, and even very small feeder goldfish.

# Small Eyed Rays
## Antenna Rays

Young specimens are especially delicate, and require extremely good water quality, no tankmates, and a quiet aquarium. Adult specimens are also relatively quiet rays, and are not seen constantly searching the substrate and aquarium for food like other species. Even large specimens are not as adept at blowing through the substrate to find food, so care must be taken to avoid overfeeding.

The common antenna ray's tail is very delicate. In our experience newly imported specimens with a damaged tail often die. If the tail is kinked or damaged towards the end it may break off and heal, or it may heal intact, leaving a small bump, or "knuckle" where the damage occurred.

However, if the tail is damaged, bent, or kinked closer to the body, especially where it changes from white to white and black, it rarely heals, and eventually falls off. Once this occurs the ray often dies. The cause of death is unknown, but may be related to infection entering through the broken end of the tail. Well-acclimated specimens seem less delicate.

Long-term specimens in our collection have lost tail sections without dying. The common antenna ray's tail can easily be damaged by objects in the tank. Rocks, driftwood, or even aquarium equipment can catch the tail,

*The very long-tailed antenna rays are among the most delicate of aquarium occupants. Here two species for comparison: left, the black-tailed antenna ray, a dwarf species; and right, the common antenna ray, which can attain a diameter of more than a metre.*

causing it to kink or break. Powerheads, lift tubes, or other equipment are equally dangerous; a specimen in our collection had its tail drawn into a powerhead intake, resulting in the tail becoming entangled with the spindle of the impeller. Accordingly members of this group are best kept in a tank without ornamentation or equipment.

Although other species of stingrays are compatible with antenna rays, other large fish may cause damage to the tail. Gravel substrates are satisfactory for antenna rays.

The black-tailed antenna ray is a rare species, and not often imported. This species seems to be less sensitive to tail injuries than the common antenna ray. Kinks in the tail are not as likely to cause the tail to fall off.

Specimens with broken tails are not at risk of dying, as are the common antenna rays. Furthermore this is the only species of stingray that commonly rests with its fin or disc margin elevated above the substrate when in good health. It is therefore an exception to the rule that elevation of the fin is a danger sign. Black-tailed antenna rays often hold their disc in strangely elevated positions. The reason for this is not known.

This species seems to be a dwarf species, because it is sexually mature at 15–18 cm / 6–7 inches (males) and is unable to eat foods

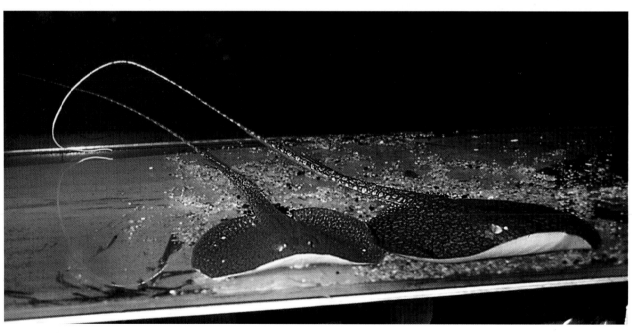

# Small Eyed Rays
## Ceja-type Rays

larger than blackworms or tubifex worms. Moreover it is not large enough to turn over gravel looking for worms, so uneaten worms will soon colonize tank substrates.

Prior to feeding more worms, the substrate should be disturbed to see if worms are present. If so, the substrate should be agitated to free the worms into the water where they can be eaten by the rays. Unfortunately, varied food species for this ray are difficult to find because of the small mouth size.

It is our experience that this species does not survive as long as other species in captivity, and this is possibly due to nutritional deficiencies resulting from a limited dietary range.

### Ceja-type Rays

These rays appear to do best in very soft water. In addition their skin is thinner and more delicate than in large-eyed rays, and they seem to be sensitive to irritation from substrates. The ceja, (the name means "eyebrow" in Spanish) receives its name from the dark markings in front of each eye which resemble eyebrows.

The manzana ("apple" in Spanish) ray, a morph of the ceja ray, is so named because its shape resembles the vertical cross-section of an apple, the tail being the stem. When kept over various substrates, ceja rays in our collection have thrived for short periods, and then developed fungal infections and died.

This appears to have been due to small abrasions occurring on the skin, which then become infected with bacteria or fungus. Ceja-type rays that have survived on substrates have developed nicks and tears in their fins. We currently maintain both types of rays on bare-bottomed tanks. This practice has avoided these problems.

In captivity ceja rays seem reluctant to eat foods other than feeder fish. Although stomach contents of wild specimens showed insects, specimens in our collection have refused all foods except live fish.

Accordingly the problem of vitamin B1 deficiency due to thiaminase must be avoided. It is our practice to add one 100mg tablet of vitamin B1 monthly to the water system of all fish that are exclusively fish-eaters. If the aquarist has access to live fish other than goldfish, it is highly recommended that a variety of live fish be offered.

Feeding live fish to rays risks introducing parasites or diseases carried by the feeder fish, so these species are best kept separately to reduce the risk to other fish.

It has been our experience that ceja rays and china rays may thrive for months, gaining

# Small Eyed Rays
## China Rays

*A light and a dark morph of the ceja ray.*

weight and feeding actively, only to die suddenly without explanation. Although we believe that these deaths are caused by the limited nutritional value of feeder goldfish, no definite cause has been found.

These species of rays do not chase down or actively hunt their food. Instead, they are ambush feeders, lying in wait in the aquarium until a fish swims past them. They then pounce on the fish, sucking it under their disc and into their mouth with water currents. Ceja rays do not attack fish unless the prey passes extremely close, or actually touches the front edge of the disc margin.

There is an area we call the "trigger zone", located on the front of the disc margin, which is sensitive to touch or motion. Until the feeder fish approaches or touches this trigger zone, the rays will remain motionless.

Ceja rays generally do not attack fish that approach on either side, only fish that approach the trigger zone at the front of the disc.

Specimens often prefer to adhere to vertical aquarium walls, waiting for fish to swim near. They then draw the prey under their disc, manipulating the feeder fish towards the mouth with water currents.

Although fascinating to observe, these rays generally do not do well in communal aquariums because of their specialized feeding requirements, and are best kept alone, as they cannot compete for food with aggressive fish. They are completely non-aggressive, and do not bite or bother other specimens.

### China Rays

These odd stingrays are similar in shape to the ceja rays, but differ in that their "trigger zone" is completely round, rather than heart-shaped. The origin of the name "china" is not known, but is believed to be based on the similarity of the shape of the ray to a Chinese hat. Like ceja rays, china rays do not attack

# Large Eyed Rays
## The Otorongo Group

fish unless the prey passes extremely close, or actually touches the "trigger zone" at the front of the disc margin. They too are ambush feeders, eating only live fish in captivity.

When resting quietly, they often undulate the caudal margin of the disc. They are very quiet rays, remaining in one location in the aquarium for long periods. However, when live fish are added to the aquarium they will aggressively ambush fish that swim near them. They can grow very large, and some reports indicate that they can exceed two metres / 78 inches.

China rays are also sensitive to substrates. When kept on sand or gravel, their disc margin often becomes frayed and damaged. When offered a bare area and an area with gravel in an aquarium, our specimens preferred a bare bottom.

China rays, like ceja rays, do not readily thrive in captivity. This may be due to the limited diet available. It is recommended that, whenever possible, other types of live fish be added in addition to feeder goldfish, and vitamin B1 be added to the water to avoid vitamin B1 deficiency.

Coly rays (coly means tail in Spanish) are nearly identical to china rays, but have a faint pattern. China rays have no pattern: they are a uniform sand colour, and may occur as dark or light morphs.

## LARGE- EYED RAYS

### The Otorongo Group

The otorongo rays are the hardiest of all freshwater stingrays. They reach a large size at maturity, often over one metre / 39 inches. Most will eat all foods, including fresh fish, frozen shrimp, and clams. They acclimate quickly, and soon become voracious feeders. They will tolerate a wide range of water

*Like all small-eyed rays, the coly rays are very difficult to maintain, and should be kept only by experienced specialists.*

*The name "china ray" has nothing to do with the provenance of the creatures; like all the rays in this book they come from tropical South America.*

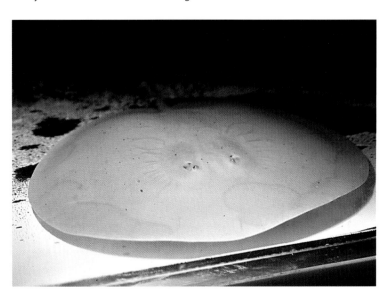

conditions, including a pH range of 6.0 to 8.0, and water with a conductivity of 400 to 500 microsiemens. Young specimens are also hardy and will grow quickly if given adequate food.

Otorongo rays are very active and aggressive fish. They often display some aggressiveness towards their own species or other rays. They can often be observed biting or chasing each other in the aquarium. It is common to see small bite marks on the fins when several are kept together. However, these small injuries are usually not serious and heal quickly.

Otorongo rays are less likely to develop infections than many other species of rays. Specimens in our collection have had severe injuries caused by other rays as well as by other aggressive large fish in the same aquarium. In each casethe injuries healed without treatment. When injuries occur, the otorongo rays do not generally stop feeding, and the wounds quickly heal.

*Otorongo rays are very rich in variants. Unfortunately these sturdy rays grow very large.*

On one occasion in our collection aggressive behaviour did cause the death of another otorongo. A dominant specimen repeatedly injured another larger but subordinate specimen. The larger specimen was removed for treatment but did not recover.

Otorongo rays are very variable in coloration and pattern, and appear in the ornamental fish trade under a variety of names. Although the differences between these morphs are subtle, they names have some consistency. (See also the identification section of the AQUALOG pictorial catalogue "Freshwater Rays".)

The husbandry of all these otorongo-type rays is the same. All are very hardy. Prolonged shipping time is less of a problem with these rays. One specimen shipped to us was discovered upside down when the box was opened. The ray was on its back in the water, gasping air and water. Once placed in the aquarium, it recovered completely.

**Tiger Rays**

Tiger stingrays are among the most challenging and delicate of the freshwater rays. These rays prefer an acid pH, in the range 6.25 to 6.5. When the pH is allowed to drift upwards to 7.0 and above their behaviour changes, and they become more quiet, feed less aggressively, and spend more time beneath the substrate.

In addition they require a warmer temperature range than other rays. While most

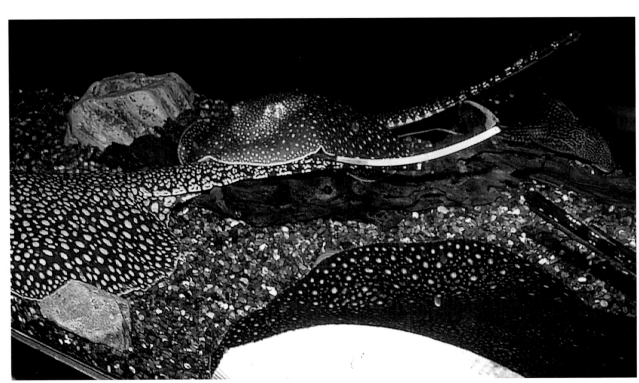

# Large Eyed Rays
## Tiger Rays

rays are active and feed aggressively within a range of 72–78F / 22–26°C, tiger rays prefer a temperature range of 80-82F / 27–28°C, never below 78F / 26°C. If kept too cool, these rays will become inactive, stop feeding, and eventually become sick and die.

When newly acquired, tiger rays seem to prefer to feed nocturnally, and remain quiet or buried in the substrate during the day. They do not readily eat feeder goldfish, and often will not accept chopped nightcrawlers for many weeks after acclimation. Even when well acclimated, they may not feed as aggressively as other rays, and do not do well in a tank with other species that are aggressive feeders. They are best kept alone or with other tiger rays. To add to the difficulty in keeping these rays, imported specimens are often large, and are badly stressed during shipping.

In addition to their more demanding husbandry requirements, tiger rays are more susceptible to infections when injured. Minor injuries, which would readily heal in other species, become seriously infected in tiger rays, requiring injectable antibiotic treatment (see page 39). An injured specimen should be removed from the aquarium and kept in isolation where it can be treated.

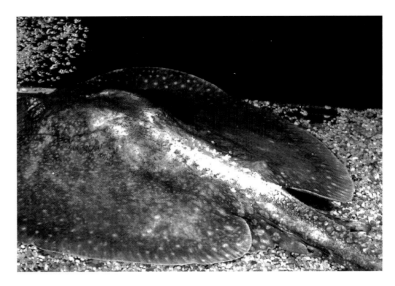

Young specimens of tiger rays are dramatically different in appearance from adults. They may be pale, with very faint markings, or they may have a golden colour to the disc. Adult coloration seems to develop at around 20–25 cm / 10–12 inches in diameter. This species does not reach sexual maturity until 45 cm / 18 inches or more.

Once well acclimated, tiger rays become less demanding as regards water conditions, and will tolerate a greater range of pH. Nonetheless these beautiful stingrays are more suitable for the advanced aquarist and

*In contrast to most other ray species, otorongo rays may seriously harm one another.*

*A young tiger ray. Remark that this specimen has fin rot. Overleaf: Adult tiger rays have a completely different appearance.*

should be considered only after the aquarist has had considerable experience with hardier species.

**The Black Rays**

Two recognized species of black stingrays are known. These are *Potamotrygon leopoldi* and *P. henlei*. The husbandry requirements of these species are identical. In fact, there is not complete agreement that these two rays are distinct species. Intermediate-type specimens are found, and in some of these it is unclear to which species they belong. The most apparent difference between these two species is that in *P. henlei* the ocelli are pale yellow in colour rather than white, and extend to the edge of the disc margin.

Furthermore in *P.henlei* the yellow markings appear on the edge ventral surface as well. In *P. leopoldi* the ocelli are white, do not extend to the edge of the disc margin, and are not present on the ventral surface. Also, *P.leopoldi* tend to be larger than *P.henlei* when imported, although this may not necessarily indicate a different maximum size in nature.

These rays are very hardy. They adapt quickly to captivity, and soon become aggressive feeders. They are compatible with other rays, but will often exhibit mildly aggressive behaviour. They will eat all foods, including frozen and fresh fish. Some specimens have even been observed to eat pelleted foods intended for other fish. *Potamotrygon leopoldi* has been bred in captivity. Sexually mature specimens are usually over 45 cm / 18 inches in diameter.

Specimens that have been badly stressed during shipping sometimes show an unusual variation in the ocelli. The white or yellow markings seem to "run" or move. As the specimen returns to normal heath, the ocelli return to normal.

**Motoro Rays**

Motoro rays are among the most commonly imported freshwater rays. They are highly

*An adult tiger ray.*

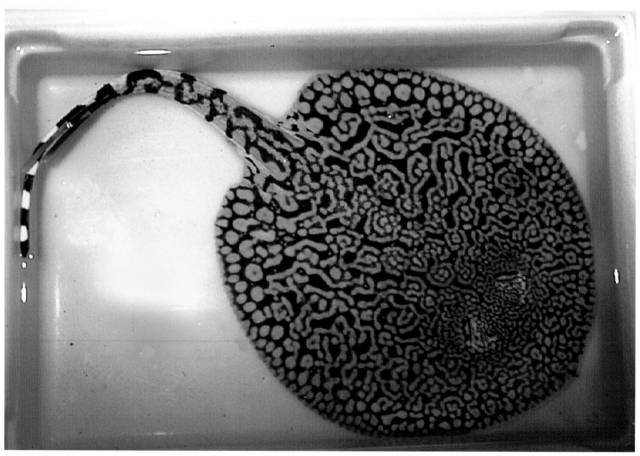

# Large Eyed Rays
## Motoro Rays

*Below: Potamotrygon leopoldi is thought to be endemic to the Rio Xingu. It is possible that the specific status of this black ray may be questioned at some time in the future, in which case it will become a synonym of P. henlei.*

*photo: F.Teigler/A.C.S.*

polymorphic, and have a widespread distribution. They are known to be very hardy, and are also said to be more aggressive with their sting than other rays. Tropical fish exporters state that motoro rays will occasionally attempt to sting when netted.

# Large Eyed Rays
## The Black Rays

The black rays, Potamotrygon henlei and P.leopoldi, are distinguished from each other on the basis of the ventral markings and details of the dorsal pattern.
In P.leopoldi (centre) the underside of the body disc is unspotted, while in P.henlei the spotted pattern of the dorsal surface continues onto the edge of the underside of the disc (below). But because intermediates are known as well, it is questionable whether they are indeed two separate species. The black rays are sturdy and durable aquarium occupants, which have already been bred on a number of occasions.

# Large Eyed Rays
## Reticulatus-, Laticeps- and Histrix-Rays

This species is also that most commonly bred in captivity. Sexual maturity is reached at a relatively small size, sometimes 25 to 30 cm / 10-12 inches. This allows captive breeding in relatively small aquaria. Field observations indicate that size at sexual maturity varies from one river system to another. In one area, 40 cm / 16 inch males have been noted to be immature, while in another area 25cm / 10 inch males are fully mature.

Motoro rays will thrive under a wide range of water conditions, with a pH of 6.0 to 8.0, as well as moderately hard to hard water. They are aggressive feeders, and will eat any small fish in an aquarium.

One collector has reported that a motoro killed and ate a smaller motoro. They eat all varieties of live foods, as well as pieces of fresh fish and even pelleted foods.

**Reticulatus, Laticeps and Histrix Rays**

Also among the commonest of imported rays, these species are highly polymorphic. Although not always as hardy as motoro rays, these species will thrive under most aquarium conditions.

Very small or newborn stingrays are often imported under the name of "teacup rays" and these are usually sold as juvenile specimens of these same three species. But, however, they belong often to completely different species. For example, *P. laticeps* is an objective synoym of *P. motoro* (fide Rosa, 1985). You will learn everything on these matters in the determination / pictorial AQUALOG „Freshwater Rays".

As with any very small stingray, "teacup" rays should be maintained in a quiet environment where competition for food is minimal. They will reach adult size at about 50 cm / 20 inches, and reach sexual maturity at about 25-30 cm / 10-12 inches. As with most

*The name "motoro ray" is a blanket term for several different stingray species.*
*photo: E.Schraml/A.C.S. archives*

# Epilogue
## Looking to the Future

*This page and P.59, top: Even where they are not particularly closely related, ray species tend all to be "tarred with the same brush" by aquarists, on account of their predominantly brown basic coloration. They are commonly imported as juveniles and the temptation to buy them is great. But please always remember that these cute little baby rays grow into substantial animals that need a considerable amount of space. Moreover such juveniles are essentially suitable only for the experienced ray-keeper, as they are far more delicate than half-grown specimens.*

*photos: P.59 top: F.Schäfer; P.58 top: A.C.S. archives; P.58 bottom: H.-F. Schmidt-Knaatz.*

common rays, they are generally compatible with other rays and with other fish that are too small to be eaten.

**Looking to the Future**

In this guide we have endeavoured to cover the practical aspects of the maintenance and breeding of freshwater stingrays.

The immensely complex topic of systematics has, by contrast, been deliberately omitted. In the near future an AQUALOG pictorial catalogue will be published, in which all the freshwater stingray species known to date will be portrayed. This pictorial catalogue will also contain an identification key which will explain how the different species can be recognised and given their correct names.

Freshwater stingray species from other continents will also be covered fully in this pictorial catalogue. For example, there are very beautiful species of freshwater stingrays from Asia that remain relatively small and about whose aquarium care practically nothing is known, so that we have not dealt

# Epilogue
## Looking to the Future

Right: Potamotrygon histrix, the first South American freshwater stingray to be scientifically described.

*Right: Potamotrygon histrix, the first South American freshwater stingray to be scientifically described.*

with these fishes here. And there are also freshwater rays that live in North and Central America, in Australia and Africa. Not all are stingrays.

They include exciting creatures such as the guitar rays and sawfishes, which also belong to the ray group. Finally, this AQUALOG pictorial catalogue will also contain a complete register of P-numbers. We invite you to be so good as to read the preview of this book on page 61.

*In the past the scientific description of freshwater stingrays was often performed from drawings, without voucher specimens being deposited in a museum. It is often virtually impossible to correlate such descriptions with living specimens, as is the case, for example, with Elipesurus spinicauda Jardine & Schomburgk (in Schomburgk, 1843), depicted below*

PLATE 2

*Elipesurus spinicauda.*

## Biotopes in South America

*Sandbank in the Rio Araguaia, a typical habitat of freshwater stingrays.*                    photo: H.-G.Evers

*These creatures are also found in fast-flowing stretches of river with stony substrates, as seen here in the upper Raudales of Mavicure, Rio Inirida,*
*upper Orinoco drainage (Colombia). Uwe Werner caught Potamotrygon motoro here.*                    photo: U.Werner

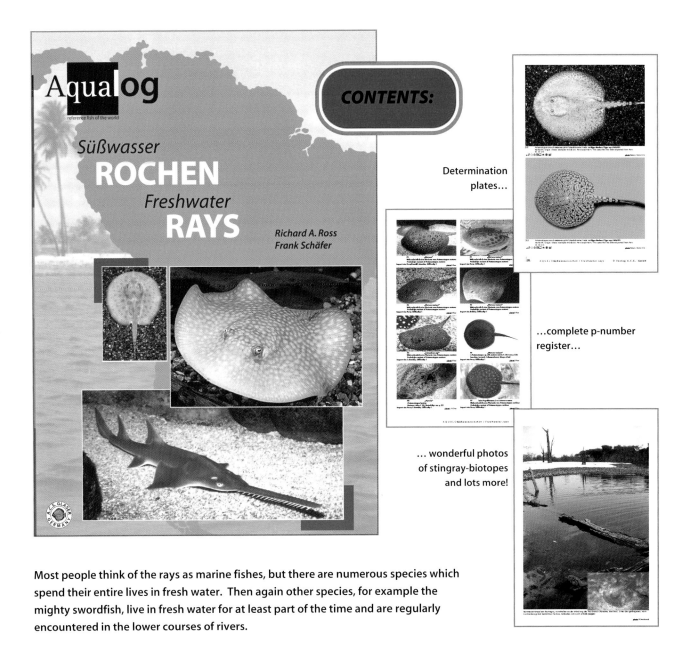

**CONTENTS:**

Determination plates...

...complete p-number register...

... wonderful photos of stingray-biotopes and lots more!

*Süßwasser*
**ROCHEN**
*Freshwater*
**RAYS**

Richard A. Ross
Frank Schäfer

Most people think of the rays as marine fishes, but there are numerous species which spend their entire lives in fresh water. Then again other species, for example the mighty swordfish, live in fresh water for at least part of the time and are regularly encountered in the lower courses of rivers.

This AQUALOG volume represents the first comprehensive publication in the popular literature to cover all the rays living in fresh and brackish water, with full coverage of:

- the sawfishes (Pristidae)
- the guitarfishes (Rhinobatidae)
- the South American freshwater stingrays (Potamotrygonidae)

as well as all the representatives of the electric rays (Torpediniformes), eagle rays, mantas, etc (Myliobatidae), and whiptail stingrays (Dasyatidae) that are known to enter fresh or brackish water.

An identification key for all the species is provided.

The aquaristically significant freshwater stingrays are depicted in colour photos illustrating a never-before-seen panoply of species and colour varieties. All the other species are likewise illustrated as never before.

Splendid biotope photos from the natural habitats of these rays round off this superlative volume.

This AQUALOG thus represents an indispensable work of reference work anyone interested in rays - aquarists, zoological gardens, scientists, and divers.

# The AQUALOG - System
## Information and Description

### AQUALOG Lexicon

The **AQUALOG** team has set itself the goal to catalogue all known ornamental fishes of the world – and this task will, of course, take several years, as there are over 40,000 fish species.

Compiling an **AQUALOG**lexicon, we take a certain group of fishes, label all known species with code-numbers, look for the newest results of fish research about natural distribution, features and maintenance of the fishes and try to get the best photographs, often from the most remote parts of the world.

Our ingenious code-number-system labels every species with its own individual code-number which the fish keeps even if a scientific re-naming occurs.

And not only the species gets a number, also each variety, distinguishing locality, colour, and breeding form.

This system makes every fish absolutely distinct for everybody. With it, international communication is very easy, because a simple number crosses almost all language barriers.

This is an advantage not only for dealers, but for hobbyists, too, and thus for all people involved in the aquarium hobby.

Again and again, new fish species are discovered or new varieties bred. Consequently, the number of fishes assigned to a certain group changes constantly and information from available specialist literature is only reliable within certain time limits. Thus, an identification lexicon that is up-to-date today is outdated after as little as one year.

To give aquarists an identification 'tool' that stays up-to-date for many years, we developed our ingenious patented code-number system.

When going to press, our books contain all fishes that are known to that date. All newly discovered or bred species are regularly published as either supplements or as so-called "stickups" in **AQUALOG**news.

These supplementary peel-back stickers can be attached to the empty pages in the back of the books.

As you can see, we provide the latest information from specialists for hobbyists. Over the years, your **AQUALOG** books will 'grow' to a complete encyclopaedia on ornamental fishes, a beautiful lexicon that is never outdated and easy to use.

### AQUALOG*news*

**AQUALOG***news* is the first international newspaper for aquarists, published in four-colour print, available in either German or English language and full of the latest news from the aquatic world.

The following rubrics are included:Top Ten, Brand New, Evergreens, Technics, Terraristics, Fish Doctor and Flora. Further, there are travel accounts, breeding reports, stories about new and well-known fish etc.

The news gives us the opportunity to be up-to-date, because up to one week before going to press, we can include reports and the 'hottest' available information.

This way, every six weeks a newspaper for friends of the aquarium hobby is published that makes sure to inform you about the latest 'arrivals' waiting for you at your local pet shop.

**AQUALOG***news* can be subscribed to and contains 40 supplementary stickers for your AQUALOG books in 12 issues. You can subscribe to the news either via your local pet shop or directly at the publishers.

Issues without stickups (print run: 80,000) are available at well-sorted pet shops. The newspaper also informs you about newly published supplements.

### AQUALOG *Special*

The *Specials* series is not intended to repeat all the things that were already known twenty years ago, like 'how to build your own aquarium' – something, probably nobody practises anymore, because there is no need to do so.

We provide the latest and most important information on fish keeping and tending: precisely and easily understandable.

We want to offer advice that helps you to avoid mistakes – and help your fishes to live a healthy life.

We intend to win more and more friends for our beautiful and healthy (because stress-reducing!) hobby.

Order our new free catalogue, where all our previous books and the ones in preparation are shown and described.

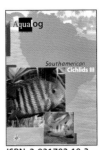

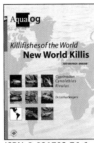

# Index